T0129193

The Windows 10 Accessibility Handbook: Supporting Windows Users with Special Visual, Auditory, Motor, and Cognitive Needs

ISBN-13 (pbk): 978-1-4842-1732-0

ISBN-13 (electronic): 978-1-4842-1733-7

Trademarked names, logos, and images may appear in this book. Rather than use a trademark symbol with every occurrence of a trademarked name, logo, or image we use the names, logos, and images only in an editorial fashion and to the benefit of the trademark owner, with no intention of infringement of the trademark.

The use in this publication of trade names, trademarks, service marks, and similar terms, even if they are not identified as such, is not to be taken as an expression of opinion as to whether or not they are subject to proprietary rights.

While the advice and information in this book are believed to be true and accurate at the date of publication, neither the authors nor the editors nor the publisher can accept any legal responsibility for any errors or omissions that may be made. The publisher makes no warranty, express or implied, with respect to the material contained herein.

Managing Director: Welmoed Spahr
Lead Editor: Gwenan Spearing
Technical Reviewer: Kathleen Anderson
Editorial Board: Steve Anglin, Pramila Balen, Louise Corrigan, Jim DeWolf, Jonathan Gennick, Robert Hutchinson, Celestin Suresh John, Michelle Lowman, James Markham, Susan McDermott, Matthew Moodie, Jeffrey Pepper, Douglas Pundick, Ben Renow-Clarke, Gwenan Spearing
Coordinating Editor: Melissa Maldonado
Copy Editor: Tiffany Taylor
Compositor: SPi Global
Indexer: SPi Global
Artist: SPi Global

Distributed to the book trade worldwide by Springer Science+Business Media New York, 233 Spring Street, 6th Floor, New York, NY 10013. Phone 1-800-SPRINGER, fax (201) 348-4505, e-mail orders-ny@springer-sbm.com, or visit www.springer.com. Apress Media, LLC is a California LLC and the sole member (owner) is Springer Science + Business Media Finance Inc (SSBM Finance Inc). SSBM Finance Inc is a **Delaware** corporation.

For information on translations, please e-mail rights@apress.com, or visit www.apress.com.

Apress and friends of ED books may be purchased in bulk for academic, corporate, or promotional use. eBook versions and licenses are also available for most titles. For more information, reference our Special Bulk Sales–eBook Licensing web page at www.apress.com/bulk-sales.

Any source code or other supplementary materials referenced by the author in this text is available to readers at www.apress.com. For detailed information about how to locate your book's source code, go to www.apress.com/source-code/.

The Windows 10 Accessibility Handbook

Supporting Windows Users with Special Visual, Auditory, Motor, and Cognitive Needs

Mike Halsey

Apress®

Contents at a Glance

Contents

About the Author

Mike Halsey is the author of more than a dozen books on Microsoft Windows, including many *Troubleshooting* books such as *Windows 10 Troubleshooting* (Apress, 2015). He was first awarded a Microsoft Most Valuable Professional (MVP) in 2011.

Based in Sheffield (UK), Mike gives many talks on how to get the very best from Microsoft Windows. He makes help, how-to, and support videos under the brands *PC Support.tv* and *Windows.do*. You can follow Mike on Facebook, Twitter, and YouTube by searching for *PCSupportTV*.

About the Technical Reviewer

Kathleen Anderson was first honored with the Microsoft MVP award in October 2001. She has worked with FrontPage since 1997 and Expression Web since Version 1, and has worked in the IT field for over 30 years. Kathleen retired from the state of Connecticut after 25 years of service, and relocated to the beach in Oak Island, North Carolina. She served as the Core-CT Webmaster (www.core-ct.state.ct.us), and chaired the Connecticut's Committee on Web Site Accessibility. She owns a web design company, Spider Web Woman Designs (www.spiderwebwoman.com). She was a technical editor on *Windows 10 Primer, Windows 10 Revealed, Microsoft Expression Web 4 in Depth*, and *Sams Teach Yourself Microsoft Expression Web 4, Second Edition*. She is known in some circles as the "FrontPage Database Wizard Queen" and in others as the "Accessibility Diva" and is a member of the International Association of Accessibility Professionals.

CHAPTER 1

Introducing Accessibility in Windows 10

We've all experienced difficulty using our PCs. Whether it's losing the mouse cursor on the screen and shaking the mouse vigorously to try to find it, or squinting to read text that's too small, usability problems abound in computing. This isn't helped by the fact that as a population, we're all getting older, living longer, and increasingly looking to the Internet as a means to keep in touch with friends and family, access public services, shop, and have fun.

If you have less than perfect eyesight or hearing or your hands are a little shaky, using a PC can sometimes be a frustrating experience. Jiggle the mouse a little, and all your windows disappear from the screen. Press the Shift or Ctrl key too many times, and the entire way the keyboard works changes. Set your resolution and desktop scaling incorrectly, and finding a button or link can take forever. And not being able to hear the PC properly means you may miss an important notification.

For people with disabilities and impairments, the challenges are greater. If you can't physically see the screen, how can you do something as simple as get online? And if you're unable to use a keyboard and mouse, typing a web address can seem like a distant goal.

Microsoft Windows has long included features aimed at making your PC, laptop, tablet, and smartphone more accessible and easier to use. With Windows 10, these tools and features are mature and comprehensive, while also being straightforward for the people who need them most.

No matter what your specific situation, from color-blindness to dyslexia, poor eyesight or hearing impairments, shaky hands, poor coordination or more severe disabilities, in this book I guide you through how to make Windows 10 easy to use on whatever device you want to use it on.

If you're supporting people who find PC use difficult, this book details how to understand the needs of different types of PC users and how to set up systems to accommodate them. Using PCs may be a challenge for some, but it doesn't have to be a problem.

What Is Windows 10 Accessibility?

The *Ease of Access tools* in Windows 10 comprise a suite of utilities, each with a specific goal and aimed at solving a specific problem. These aren't just tools that always work in isolation, however, and they're not by any means the only accessibility functions available; the operating system contains utilities that might be generally considered mainstream but that can also aid accessibility considerably.

But what are the main accessibility tools in Windows 10, and what challenges are they intended to solve?

Narrator

The *Narrator* is the spoken voice of your PC, reading not just text in documents and on web pages, but also menu options, window names and features, and any other text available onscreen. It operates in several ways: it can read text automatically in a window when it opens, and you can also scan text with your mouse cursor or finger.

Magnifier

Often, people find window features, links, and buttons either too small to see or, in the case of many web pages, too faint to see. This is where the Magnifier comes in, and it too has several modes of operation. You can use it as you would move a magnifying glass across a page, or you can dock it onscreen, providing a larger, magnified view.

High-Contrast Themes

Windows 10 is designed to look aesthetically pleasing, but this doesn't always make things easy to see or help you focus on the task at hand. The high-contrast themes can create clear delimiters between open windows and dialogs and can help make everything on your screen easier to read.

Closed Captioning

You're used to being able to turn on subtitles for programs on your TV or for movies you're watching on Blu-ray or DVD. Windows 10 includes this feature, but it's not supported in all apps. The Film & TV app, however, lets you automatically turn on closed captioning for all videos that support it.

Keyboard Enhancements

Keyboards can be tricky to use sometimes, not just because keypress combinations can use two or even three keys, but also because keyboards can be quite wide. Functions exist to make it easy to use multiple-key combinations, to handle slow keypresses, and more.

Mouse Enhancements

At the beginning of this chapter, I highlighted the all-too-common case of losing the mouse cursor onscreen. We've all done it. Windows 10 includes options to prevent this from happening, making it easier to both find and follow the cursor. You can also use your keyboard's cursor keys instead of the mouse if you need to.

Concentration Enhancements

There can sometimes be a lot happening onscreen, and enhancements exist to help you focus more easily on the task at hand and concentrate on getting your work done.

Additional Enhancements

Many features are built in to Windows 10 that aren't aimed at improving accessibility but that can greatly enhance your PC's ease of use and improve your experience, such as touch zoom controls and laptop trackpad swipes.

Settings Sync

Once you have set up your PC as you want it, assuming you are signed in to Windows 10 using an account that can sync across devices—such as a Microsoft account or domain or Azure Active Directory—your accessibility settings can be set to synchronize across all the PCs you sign in to. This even includes new PCs that you haven't used before; you'll see your accessibility settings sync to those PCs shortly after you first sign in.

Who Can Benefit from Accessibility in Windows 10?

Clearly, there's a lot in Windows 10 that can be used to make your experience more enjoyable and productive. You can use some or all of these features together, and everything can be customized to your own needs—but who might benefit from such features?

Here I'm talking more to people who will be supporting users in a company environment or perhaps in their homes. There's a common misconception that the Ease of Access options in Windows 10 have been put there to make life simpler for the disabled, but this isn't actually the case.

Of course, if you are blind or physically impaired in some way, it's clear that features such as the Narrator and keyboard, mouse, and touch enhancements can help. Also, if a person has a neurological or cognitive disability, making it easier for them to focus on a task can be of enormous benefit.

It doesn't stop there, however—huge numbers of different types of people can benefit from making Windows 10 easier to use. The elderly can benefit from the ease-of-access features. This planet has an aging population, and as we get older, we tend to slow down and can find it more difficult to perform intricate tasks.

The young aren't excluded, either. Poor eyesight, color-blindness, dyslexia, hearing problems, motor difficulties, and concentration problems can hit anybody at any age. You may not think you need help or support, but that doesn't mean making things slightly bigger onscreen or using a more suitable color scheme won't help you focus more easily on your work or help you enjoy using your PC more.

Finally, there are people like me and, possibly, you, who occasionally lose the mouse cursor onscreen and find it frustrating to have to wiggle the mouse to find it again.

So who can benefit from the Ease of Access features in Windows 10? Quite literally *every single* Windows 10 user, be they on a desktop PC, laptop, tablet, or smartphone. Everyone has the potential to benefit from the Ease of Access features in some way, which makes the benefits to both individuals and businesses absolutely enormous.

Accessibility Begins at Sign-In

With Windows 10, your accessibility options begin at the sign-in screen, where you choose your user account and type your password or PIN. When you start a Windows 10 PC, the sign-in screen is the first thing to appear; refer to Figure 1-1. In the bottom-left corner of the screen, and only if you have more than one user account set up on the PC, a list of accounts is visible. In the center of the screen is (top to bottom) your user avatar (photo), your name, the account name you sign in with (such as your Microsoft Account e-mail address), a password or PIN input box, and, below that, a link to additional sign-in options if you have set them up on the PC. This can include features such as a picture password you can draw on the screen.

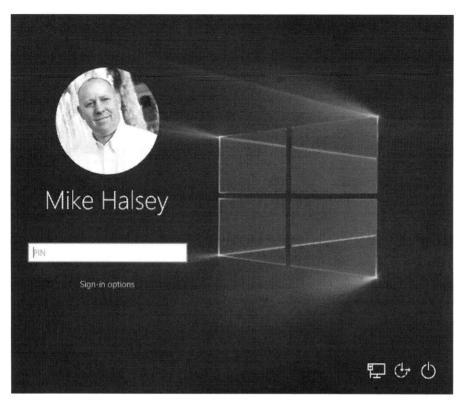

Figure 1-1. *The Ease of Access icon on the sign-in screen is in the bottom-right corner of your screen, just to the left of the power icon*

▦ **Note**   The sign-in screen on a Windows 10 Mobile smartphone is different. Only if you have set a security PIN, the screen presents a numeric keyboard that stretches the width of the screen and about a third of the way up the screen from the bottom. In the bottom-left corner is a light button that illuminates the numbers on the keypad as you press them, making it easier to see which number you have pressed.

In the bottom-right corner of the screen are three icons. From left to right, these show your current network connection status, which allows you to connect to a Wi-Fi network; the Ease of Access icon, which I talk about shortly; and a power icon.

The Ease of Access icon is a dashed semicircle with two intersecting arrows. Selecting it presents a pop-up menu with the options available; refer to Figure 1-2.

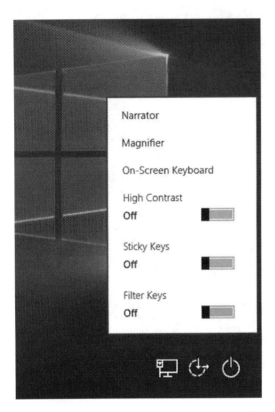

Figure 1-2. Selecting the Ease of Access icon on the sign-in screen presents a pop-up menu of options. Top to bottom: Narrator, Magnifier, onscreen keyboard, high contrast, sticky keys, and filter keys

The options that appear in the Ease of Access pop-up menu are, from top to bottom, links to activate the Narrator, Magnifier and onscreen keyboard, and then toggle switches to turn on and off the high-contrast theme, sticky keys, and filter keys. I discuss all of these later in the book.

Managing Accessibility in the Settings App

Once you are signed in to Windows 10, you're presented with the desktop, which has a Windows button in the bottom-left corner. You can select this button to open the Start menu; refer to Figure 1-3.

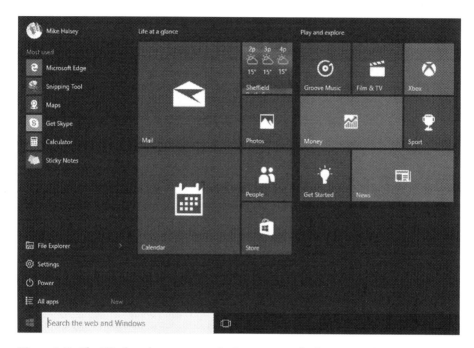

Figure 1-3. *The Windows button opens the Start menu, which presents, directly above it, these buttons: All Apps, Power, and Settings, and File Explorer as you move upward*

When the Start menu opens, its bottom-left corner, directly above the Windows key, features links (as you move upward) for All Apps, which opens a vertical scrolling list of all your installed apps; Power, which opens a fly-out menu with the Sleep, Shut Down, and Restart options; Settings and File Explorer. To open the Ease of Access options, select the Settings icon.

Using the Start Menu on a Windows 10 Tablet

If you are using a tablet, you access the Settings icon in a different way, because the Start menu side panel containing the Settings option is hidden (refer to Figure 1-4). Once you have selected the Windows key, select the top-left corner of the screen to open a new menu panel with the Settings icon available, as described previously. The icon at top left is called a *hamburger icon*, because its three horizontal lines resemble a hamburger.

Figure 1-4. The Settings icon is hidden in the Start menu on Windows 10 tablets. Once you have opened the Start menu, you must select an icon at top-left on your screen to display the Settings icon

Using the Start Menu on a Windows 10 Mobile Smartphone

Again, things are slightly different on a smartphone. From the top of your screen, swipe downward with your finger to reveal the Action Center. Just below the signal and battery information at the very top of the screen is a row of four square buttons. The button on the far right *should* open the Settings app; refer to Figure 1-5. I say *should* because these buttons can be customized, so your carrier or another person from whom you obtained the phone might have changed them.

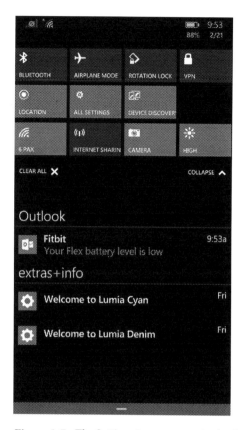

Figure 1-5. *The Settings icon appears in the Action Center in Windows 10 Mobile. Swipe downward from the top of your screen to display it*

If this is the case, directly below this row of buttons and at right on the screen is an Expand link, which displays further rows of buttons. Settings is included somewhere in the list.

The Settings App

Once open, the Settings app presents nine main categories of Windows 10 settings. This list displays as a grid of two or three rows of icons (refer to Figure 1-6) on a desktop or tablet and as a single column of icons on a Windows 10 Mobile smartphone.

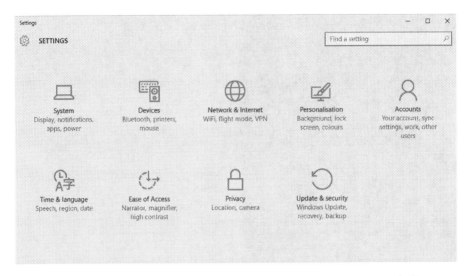

Figure 1-6. *The Settings app presents the nine main settings categories in a grid of icons across one, two, or three rows, depending on the size of the Settings window and the size of your screen*

The main categories of Settings are as follows:

- *System,* where you can find settings for power management, notifications, default apps, and your display settings

- *Devices,* where you can install and control USB, Bluetooth, and other connected devices, and manage printers

- *Network & Internet,* where you can connect to and manage Wi-Fi, wired (Ethernet), virtual private network (VPN), and other network types

- *Personalization,* where you find all the settings for your desktop look and feel, lock screen, and color scheme

- *Accounts,* where you can add, manage, and remove users on the PC, and manage your Microsoft account and PC synchronization settings

- *Time & Language,* where you can set options that depend on your region and language

- *Ease of Access,* which I detail shortly

- *Privacy,* which contains many options for helping you manage privacy on your PC

- *Update & Security,* which contains the settings for Windows Update, the Windows Defender antivirus software, File History backup, and Windows 10 recovery and reset options

The Ease of Access icon is the seventh icon in the list. Selecting it reveals a dual panel of categories on the left side of the window, and options for that category on the right. Note that if you are using a Windows 10 Mobile smartphone, you just have the categories and can select these for their individual settings. The categories (refer to Figure 1-7) are Narrator, Magnifier, High Contrast, Closed Captions, Keyboard, Mouse, and Other Options.

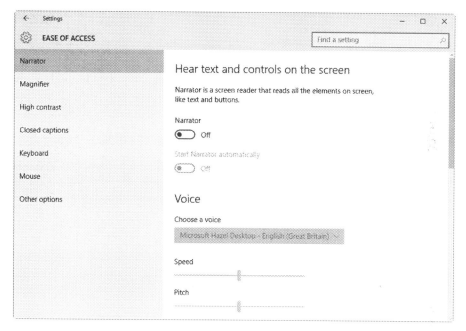

Figure 1-7. *The Ease of Access settings show seven main categories on the left side of the window, running top to bottom. The right side of the window shows the settings for the currently selected category*

▓ **Note** It's worth noting that, as I mentioned earlier, Windows 10 includes many settings that can be extremely useful in making your PC easier to use but that aren't designated as Ease of Access. Throughout this book, I show you where to find these and how to use them.

There are two different ways to select the category of setting you wish to change:

- Click or tap the relevant category with your mouse or finger.

- With the first category selected, use the keyboard up and down cursor keys to move to the category you want, and press the Enter key to select it.

The right side of the Settings app contains all the settings available in that particular category. These appear in a vertically scrollable panel and can include the following elements:

- *Switches* that let you turn an element on or off

- *Drop-down menus* you can select or highlight and then press Enter to display a list of available options (you can use the cursor keys in these menus to select items, or click them)

- *Icons* displaying different options (such as mouse cursor types)

- *Sliders* that you can move left or right to change a setting (such as the cursor width or voice pitch)

- *Buttons* such as Apply (to confirm your settings) and Restore (to undo changes you made)

At top right in the Settings app is a search box, in which you can type plain-language searches to find the setting you want. When you are searching, the entire Settings app becomes a vertical, scrollable list of results.

When you have already opened a Settings category, a Back button appears in the top-left corner of the window. Directly below this is a Settings icon that, when selected, returns you to the main Settings category screen.

Note that the search box and Back button appear at the bottom of the screen in Windows 10 Mobile, as a pop-up bar you can display by swiping upward from below the screen with a finger.

Introducing the Ease of Access Center

Almost all the settings you need to manage accessibility in Windows 10 can be found in the Settings app, but some are still in the older-style Control Panel. There are several ways to access the Control Panel and the Ease of Access Center. You can open the Start menu and begin typing **Ease of Access** to display a list of search results: the Ease of Access Center will be first. Note that the Control Panel and Ease of Access Center are not available in Windows 10 Mobile.

You can press the Windows key + X to display the administration menu. This pops up in the bottom-left corner of your screen, and the Control Panel is on the list.

You can find specific Ease of Access tools in the All Apps view of the Start menu, listed under Windows Ease of Access.

When you open the Control Panel for the first time, you are presented with its category view; refer to Figure 1-8. Ease of Access is the last category and appears toward the bottom on the right side of the window.

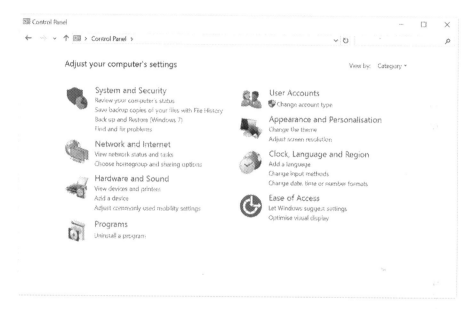

Figure 1-8. *The default Control Panel view shows the settings in categories, similar to the Settings app, but moving the cursor moves between every item available, not just the category headers*

The Ease of Access Center presents options and links as a vertically scrolling panel; refer to Figure 1-9. At the top are quick-access links to the most common controls. These include the Magnifier, the Narrator, the onscreen keyboard, and the high-contrast color scheme.

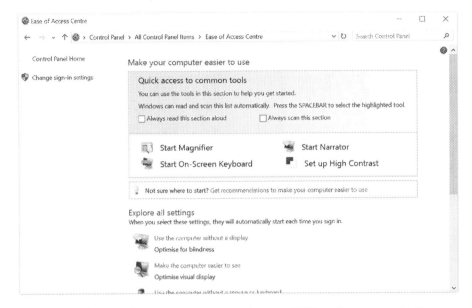

Figure 1-9. *The Ease of Access Center presents the accessibility options as a vertically scrolling panel, with quick links to the most commonly used controls highlighted at the top*

Below these quick links are the remaining settings. These are as follows:

- *Use the Computer Without a Display*: Settings to optimize your PC for people with severe visual impairments

- *Make the Computer Easier to See*: Settings that can increase the size and legibility of items onscreen

- *Use the Computer Without a Mouse or Keyboard*: Enables you to set up alternative input methods for the PC

- *Make the Mouse Easier to See*: Increases the size and changes the color of the mouse cursor

- *Make the Keyboard Easier to Use*: Activates features such as sticky keys, which make it easier to use multiple key combinations as well keys used with Shift or Ctrl

- *Use Text or Visual Alternatives for Sound*: Gives people with auditory impairments visual notification of events that usually use audio to alert the user

- *Make it Easier to Focus on Tasks*: Lets you adjust reading and typing settings

- *Make Touch and Tablets Easier to Use*: Contains settings specifically for tablets and touchscreen devices

14

Selecting each of these categories takes you to a page with the individual settings available, and there are a great many. I detail these settings throughout this book.

Summary

The accessibility settings in Windows 10 are extensive and not just aimed at narrow categories of PC users. Indeed, there are hundreds of ways in which you can customize and tweak your PC, laptop, tablet, or smartphone to make it easier to see, hear, use, and touch. Throughout this book, I show you how to use them all, and I detail where each one might be useful or relevant to you or the people you support.

CHAPTER 2

Identifying Your Needs

Now that Windows accessibility has been introduced in general terms, you may be wondering how these features are relevant to you, your colleagues, your friends, your family, or the people you support. It's fairly obvious that if somebody has a serious physical or cogitative impairment, Windows 10's accessibility features and tools can help—but what about everybody else?

This chapter takes you through some individual use cases, detailing who might benefit and how from various features and tools. This will act as your guide for how to use this book and how to find the settings you need. I want to start with some of the perhaps less-well-known use cases.

The Silver Surfer

Older PC users (whom I like to refer to as Silver Surfers) are the most obvious category of PC user to benefit from the accessibility features in the OS, after those people who have a disability. We're all getting older as a population and, as such, Silver Surfers are now online in the millions.

A broad range of features can be useful to this group of PC users, because when we get older, we find that bits of us that worked perfectly well before have suddenly given up. (If you're under 40 and reading this, you have all of this to look forward to.) Problems that older people can have include those listed in Table 2-1.

Table 2-1. *Accessibility Tools for the Elderly*

Impairment	Description	Accessibility and Other Tools
Vision	Text and icons become harder to see and read.	Desktop scaling can make items on your screen up to 350% larger.
		The Narrator can read aloud highlighted text.
		The Magnifier can make items onscreen larger.
		Underlines can be automatically added to all selectable links in Windows and your apps.
	It becomes difficult to distinguish items onscreen.	High-contrast themes can make items easier to distinguish.
		Visual options can highlight notifications and flash items to highlight them.
		Visual options can remove the desktop background.
		Visual options can increase the cursor thickness.
		The mouse cursor can be increased in size and inverted.
Hearing	Sounds, alerts, and voices become harder to hear.	Closed captioning can be activated for compatible video.
		Visual options can flash items onscreen to signal alerts.
Motor	The keyboard becomes harder to use.	Sticky Keys can reduce the need for two- and three-keypress combinations.
		Toggle Keys can alert you when you successfully press Caps Lock or Num Lock.
		Filter Keys can prevent repeated keystrokes when you press a key for too long.
		Filter Keys can make a sound when you successfully press a key.
		Underlines can be added to all links in Windows and apps.
	The mouse becomes harder to use precisely.	The mouse can be inverted and the area around it highlighted.
		The number keys on your keyboard can be used to control the cursor.
		Desktop scaling can make icons, buttons, and other items larger.
Concentration	It becomes harder to see alerts.	Notifications can be set to appear onscreen for any length of time from 5 seconds to 5 minutes.
	Using apps becomes confusing.	The desktop background can be hidden.
		Window and other animations can be disabled.

18

Workers in Busy or Noisy Environments

This may surprise you, but many of the same concentration and visual problems faced by people with cogitative impairments also affect those who work in busy or noisy environments. Working on a factory or warehouse floor can be a loud and distracting experience, and there will likely be deadlines you need to meet that can cause stress if you can't concentrate on what's happening on your PC. If you work in an environment where activities on your PC can have critical consequences, such as healthcare or fire and rescue, you can also benefit from some of Windows 10's accessibility features; see Table 2-2.

Table 2-2. *Accessibility Tools for People in Busy or Noisy Environments*

Impairment	Description	Accessibility and Other Tools
Hearing	Sounds, alerts, and voices are harder to hear.	Visual options can flash items onscreen to signal alerts.
Concentration	It becomes harder to know when alerts have arrived.	Notifications can be set to appear onscreen for any length of time from 5 seconds to 5 minutes.
	There are too many background distractions or too much noise.	The desktop background can be hidden.
		Window and other animations can be disabled.

Young Children

I know, who'd have thought that young children could benefit from using the accessibility features on PCs and tablets? When I was growing up, if I spent too long sitting in front of the television, my parents would tell me I'd get "square eyes." Although this might not be technically correct, it is true that eyestrain can be a problem for people who look at a screen too closely or for too long.

When children are young, their eyes (along with everything else) are still growing and adjusting to the world around them. As a result, eyestrain in the very young can potentially cause bigger problems for them as they grow older. Table 2-3 lists features that can help.

Table 2-3. *Accessibility Tools for Young Children*

Impairment	Description	Accessibility and Other Tools
Vision	You want to prevent eyestrain in young children.	Desktop scaling can be used to increase the size of text, icons, and apps, letting the child use apps while being further from the screen.
Coordination	You want to help children interact in more natural ways.	The various onscreen keyboards can be used to help children interact through touch and direct interaction with apps.

Color-Blindness and Dyslexia

For people who are color-blind or who are dyslexic, text and other items onscreen can be confusing or difficult to read. Table 2-4 lists useful accessibility tools.

▓ **Tip**　People with dyslexia often find that placing a yellow or blue transparent sheet over written text aids legibility. If you use a desktop PC with a separate monitor, changing the color temperature in your monitor's onscreen display settings can reproduce this effect by adding a yellow or blue hue to the screen.

Table 2-4. *Accessibility Tools for Color-blindness and Dyslexia*

Impairment	Description	Accessibility and Other Tools
Vision	Text and other items onscreen can be difficult to read and see.	Desktop scaling can make items onscreen larger and easier to read.
	Items onscreen can be difficult to distinguish from one another.	High-contrast themes can make it easier to differentiate items onscreen from one another.
		Visual options can hide the Windows desktop background.

Nearsighted and Farsighted People

Do you know somebody who wears glasses? Maybe you do, and perhaps you've been wearing them for so long that you don't even think about it anymore.

The problems of PC use for those who are nearsighted or farsighted are more than just having to squint at text and other items onscreen. Prolonged PC use can result in eyestrain and headaches for anyone. If you already have a visual impairment, no matter how slight, additional glare from looking at a PC screen through glasses can exacerbate this effect. See Table 2-5 for helpful tools.

Table 2-5. *Accessibility Tools for Nearsighted and Farsighted People*

Impairment	Description	Accessibility and Other Tools
Vision	A person is nearsighted or farsighted and wears glasses.	Desktop scaling can make items onscreen larger and easier to read at a distance, can help reduce the need for glasses when using a PC, and can also reduce eyestrain.
	Glare from a PC screen can cause headaches and eyestrain.	Using a monitor, laptop, or tablet with a matte screen can reduce glare.
		Wearing sunglasses when using a PC can reduce glare and eyestrain.
		Using a PC away from direct sunlight or strong overhead lights can reduce screen glare.

People with Motor or Coordination Difficulties and RSI

You may find that when you're using a keyboard or mouse, you're sometimes (or often) less than precise. This can be because your hands are little shaky, or perhaps because prolonged use has resulted in repetitive strain injury (RSI). As such, using a keyboard or mouse can present aches and pain in your hands, arms or back. The tools in Table 2-6 can help.

Table 2-6. *Accessibility Tools for People with Motor Difficulties*

Impairment	Description	Accessibility and Other Tools
Motor	Multiple-keypress combinations are difficult to perform.	Sticky Keys can reduce two- and three-keypress combinations to one key at a time.
	The mouse is imprecise and difficult to use.	Desktop scaling can make items onscreen larger and easier to select.
		The number pad on your keyboard can be used to control the mouse cursor when required.
		Alternative mice are available for purchase, including joysticks, trackpads, and trackballs.

Moderate to Severe Physical Impairments

I haven't forgotten! People with moderate to severe physical impairments can benefit from many accessibility features in Windows 10; see Table 2-7.

Table 2-7. *Accessibility Tools for People with Moderate to Severe Physical Impairments*

Impairment	Description	Accessibility and Other Tools
Motor	Keyboards and mice cannot be used.	Voice interaction through Speech Recognition can be used to interact with a PC, launch and control apps, and write documents.
		Cortana can be used as a digital PC assistant through Speech Recognition.
	Keyboards are difficult to use.	The onscreen keyboards can present an alternative input method.
		Sticky Keys, Toggle Keys, and Filter Keys options can make a keyboard simpler to use.
	Touchscreens are difficult to use.	Desktop scaling can make onscreen items larger and easier to select.
		The onscreen keyboard can be set to work by sliding over keys and staying on one to select it.
	The mouse can be difficult to use.	The numeric pad on a keyboard can be used as an alternative for the mouse.
		Keyboards and numeric pads with large keys are available for purchase.

Moderate to Severe Visual Impairments

Visual impairments can result in nearsightedness or farsightedness, but can also include very severe vision problems and blindness. Nobody should be excluded from the full PC experience, however, and solutions exist in Windows 10; see Table 2-8.

Table 2-8. *Accessibility Tools for People with Moderate to Severe Visual Impairments*

Impairment	Description	Accessibility and Other Tools
Vision	Blindness means a user cannot see a PC screen.	The Narrator can read aloud text, menu items, and all interface elements in Windows 10 and apps.
	Moderate visual impairments make the screen very difficult to see.	The Magnifier can greatly increase the size of text and other items onscreen to make them easier to see.
		Audible alerts for notifications and other events on a PC can be set as alternatives to visual alerts.
		High-contrast themes can be used to make items onscreen easier to see and read.

Moderate to Severe Cognitive Impairments

For people with a moderate to severe cognitive impairment, many tools exist to help in making a PC easier to use. These include some of the same utilities that can be used by people in noisy or distracting workplaces; see Table 2-9.

Table 2-9. *Accessibility Tools for People with Moderate to Severe Cognitive Impairments*

Impairment	Description	Accessibility and Other Tools
Concentration	It is difficult to concentrate on the PC and apps.	Desktop wallpaper can be disabled.
		High-contrast themes can make interface elements easier to distinguish.
		Desktop and other scaling options can make items easier to see.
		Windows and other distracting animations can be switched off.
		Notifications can be set to display for any length of time from 5 seconds to 5 minutes.
		Closed captioning can be added automatically to all compatible video.

System Administrators and Those Who Are Unsure

If you're unsure what settings might help make your Windows 10 PC, laptop, or tablet easier to use, the Ease of Access Center in the Control Panel contains a highlighted section with a Get Recommendations To Make Your Computer Easier To Use link (refer to Figure 2-1). You can run a wizard that sets up your PC automatically depending on the answers you give to a series of questions.

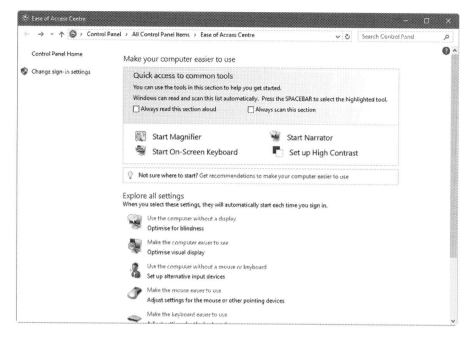

Figure 2-1. *The Ease of Access Center has a horizontal highlighted band across it, containing a link to a setup wizard*

If you are supporting other users or are a system administrator, placing a link to the Ease of Access Center on the desktop and informing users about this wizard can take the guesswork out of setting up accessibility on a PC—especially considering that everybody's needs and preferences are individual to them.

Syncing Your Settings across PCs

Once you have set up your accessibility choices on a PC, you can auto-replicate them to all the other Windows 10 PCs on which you sign in using the same Microsoft account, domain, or Azure Active Directory ID.

In the Settings app, select Accounts and then Sync Your Settings. Here you find all the synchronization options for your account, one of which is Ease of Access; refer to Figure 2-2.

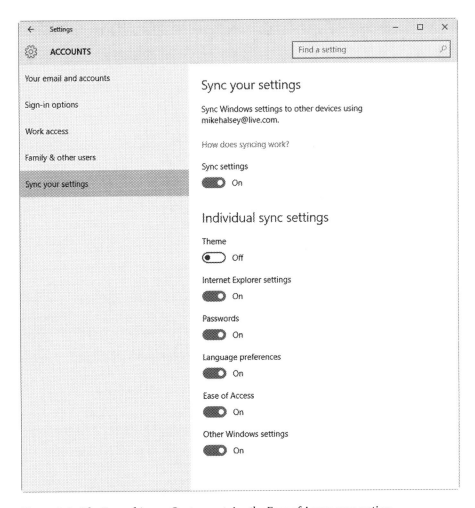

Figure 2-2. The Ease of Access Center contains the Ease of Access sync option

It's worth noting that if you are using settings such as screen scaling, you need to set this individually on each PC. But other visual settings, such as your wallpaper and theme, can be synced in the Settings app.

Summary

Accessibility in Windows 10 really is for everybody. If you haven't found while reading this chapter that you fit into a category where the accessibility features can help you, chances are that you know someone who does.

The main interface for a PC, no matter what type of device you use, is a screen. The next chapter dives straight into how you can make what's on your screen easier to read and understand.

■ ■ ■

CHAPTER 3

Reading and Understanding What's on Your Screen

When you think about it, there's an odd disparity between the way our computers communicate with us, and the way we communicate back to them. Our PCs use sight and sound as their communications interface, and we use touch to communicate back. In Chapter 7 I will show you how to make the touch interface in Windows 10 easier to use, but what happens if you have difficulty seeing what's on your PC's screen?

Cortana is a great way to interact with your PC or smartphone using your voice. You can launch apps, send e-mails, get directions, and more without ever having to touch your keyboard; and at every stage, you get audible feedback—meaning you don't need to see what's on your screen. However, Windows 10's Ease of Access features include some fantastic tools that make your PC, laptop, tablet, or smartphone considerably easier to see.

Using the Magnifier to Make the Screen Easier to See

Whereas you can use the Narrator to read aloud words and interface elements in Windows 10 and your apps, the Magnifier can be used to increase the size of items on the screen, to make them easier to see and read. When you activate the Magnifier in the Ease of Access settings, a large magnifier panel appears at the top of your screen; refer to Figure 3-1.

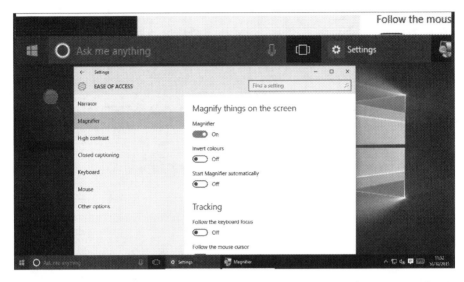

Figure 3-1. *The Magnifier displays a large magnified area at the top of your screen when it is activated*

As you move your mouse cursor around the screen, the magnified area follows you, but that's not all you can do with the Magnifier. If you move your mouse cursor into the Magnifier box itself, the cursor changes to a four-way arrow cursor. If you grab this by selecting it with your mouse, you can drag the Magnifier away from the top of the screen. It then appears as a floating window on your desktop that can be positioned anywhere (see Figure 3-2); or you can dock it to the left, right, bottom, or (again) top of the screen by moving it to one of those locations and holding the Shift key.

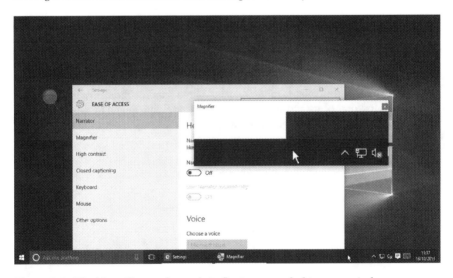

Figure 3-2. *The Magnifier can be made to float on your desktop as a window you can position anywhere*

Near the top left of your desktop is a magnifying glass icon. This is the main Magnifier control; refer to Figure 3-3.

Figure 3-3. *The Magnifier control appears as a magnifying glass icon near the top left of your desktop*

If you select this magnifying glass icon, it expands to display the full Magnifier controls; refer to Figure 3-4.

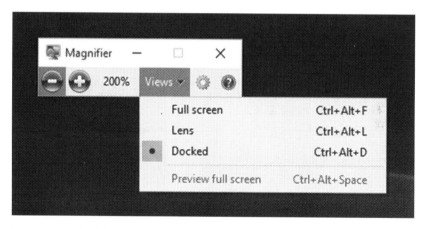

Figure 3-4. *The full Magnifier controls include, from left to right, zoom out and in buttons, a display showing the current percentage zoom level, a Views drop-down menu, a Settings icon, and a Help icon*

You can use the minus (-) and plus (+) buttons to change the zoom level of the Magnifier from 100% up to 1600%. The Views drop-down menu allows you to choose from three different views for the Magnifier:

- Full Screen (Ctrl+Alt+F) zooms your entire screen. I know people who have activated this accidentally and didn't then know how to turn it off. You can select the magnifying glass icon to open the options and deactivate it, or use the keyboard shortcut for one of the other two options.

- Lens (Ctrl+Alt+L) moves the Magnifier with your mouse so that the area under your mouse is always magnified.

- Docked (Ctrl+Alt+D) docks the Magnifier either in a floating window on your screen or to one edge of the screen.

The settings vary depending on what view you are using in the Magnifier. If you are using the Magnifier full screen or docked, you see the settings in Figure 3-5.

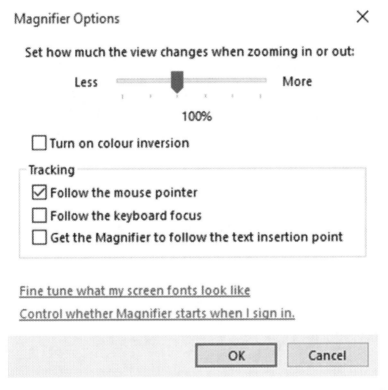

Figure 3-5. *The Full Screen and Docked settings present a slider zoom control and four check boxes*

These settings present a horizontal zoom slider and four check boxes:

- *Turn On Color Inversion*: Inverts the colors in the Magnifier to help you better distinguish the Magnifier from your desktop

- *Follow The Mouse Pointer*: Selected by default

- *Follow The Keyboard Focus*: Moves the Magnifier depending on your cursor and Tab keyboard actions

- *Get The Magnifier To Follow The Text Insertion Point*: Makes the Magnifier automatically zoom on anything you type onscreen

If you are using the Lens view for the Magnifier, the settings appear as in Figure 3-6.

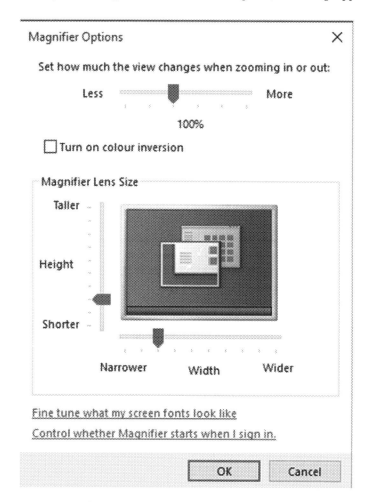

Figure 3-6. *The Magnifier settings are slightly different for the Lens view*

31

In the Lens view, you are presented with a horizontal zoom slider and Turn On Color Inversion check box. Below these is a graphic of a screen with vertical and horizontal slider controls. These allow you to change the size of the Magnifier lens window on your screen.

In the main Magnifier controls in the Settings app are additional toggle switches that can help you manage the Magnifier on your screen (refer to Figure 3-7): Invert Colors, Start Magnifier Automatically, Follow The Keyboard Focus, and Follow The Mouse Cursor.

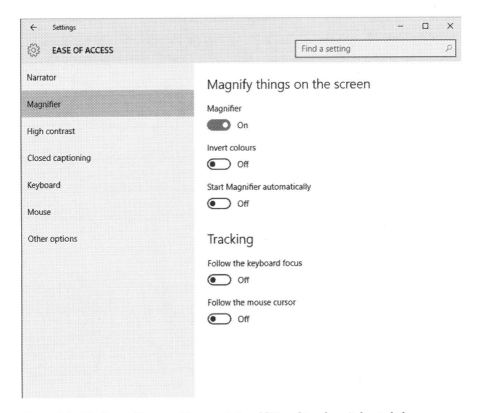

Figure 3-7. The Ease of Access settings contain additional toggle switches to help you manage the Magnifier

Using the High-Contrast Themes to Make Your Screen Easier to See

You can find the high-contrast themes in the Ease of Access settings as the third option, below the Magnifier; refer to Figure 3-8.

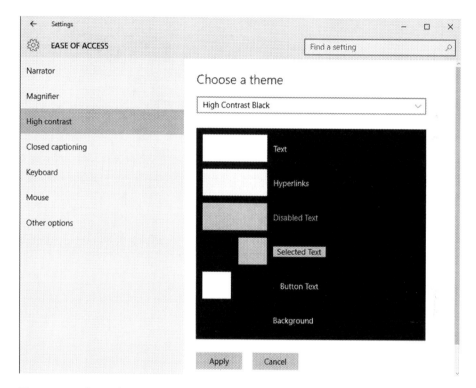

Figure 3-8. *The High Contrast settings present a drop-down menu with the different themes available. Below this is a live representation of how the theme will look*

Four high-contrast themes are available in Windows 10. You can add more if they are provided by a support organization, as I show you shortly.

You select a theme from the drop-down menu at the top of the window, below which is a live representation of how the currently selected theme will look. When you are happy with the chosen theme, select the Apply button.

If additional themes have been provided for you, or if you want to search for more themes online, open the Personalization section of the Settings app and select the Themes link. On the right side of the Settings app then appears a Theme Settings link; select it to open the Control Panel Themes window; refer to Figure 3-9.

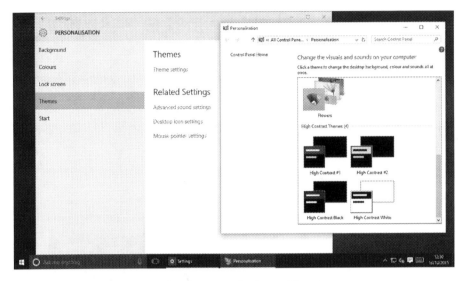

Figure 3-9. *You can manage other themes in the Control Panel*

When you have been provided with a theme, double-click, or double-tap it to open and activate it. The theme is then automatically activated; if you later change themes and want to put this theme back, the Control Panel Themes window presents a list of all your installed themes, including the high-contrast themes. At the top of this panel is a Get More Themes Online link that opens a browser window and takes you to the Themes page of the Microsoft web site.

Using the Narrator in Windows 10

Windows 10's Narrator can read aloud the content of documents, messages, and alert dialogs. It's not limited to this, however: it can help you navigate interface features, menus, options, and more.

You activate the Narrator in the Ease of Access settings. Narrator is the first option in the left panel; refer to Figure 3-10.

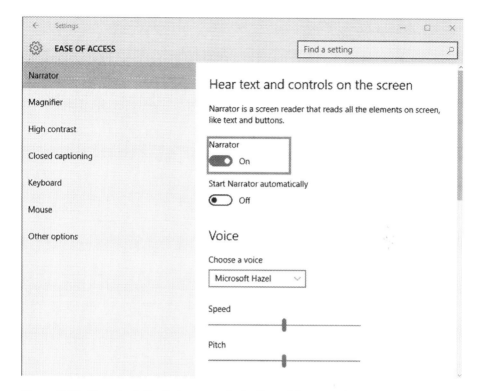

Figure 3-10. *Narrator is the first category in the Ease of Access settings*

When the Narrator is activated, whatever is currently highlighted and being read aloud by the Narrator is highlighted with an outline.

When you start the Narrator, the Narrator Settings window appears onscreen; refer to Figure 3-11. Here you can customize the Narrator to suit your personal requirements by using its options: from top to bottom, General, Navigation, Voice, and Commands. Below these are Minimize and Exit buttons. If you do not see the Narrator settings on your screen, a Narrator icon will have appeared in the System Tray on your Taskbar, select this to open the settings.

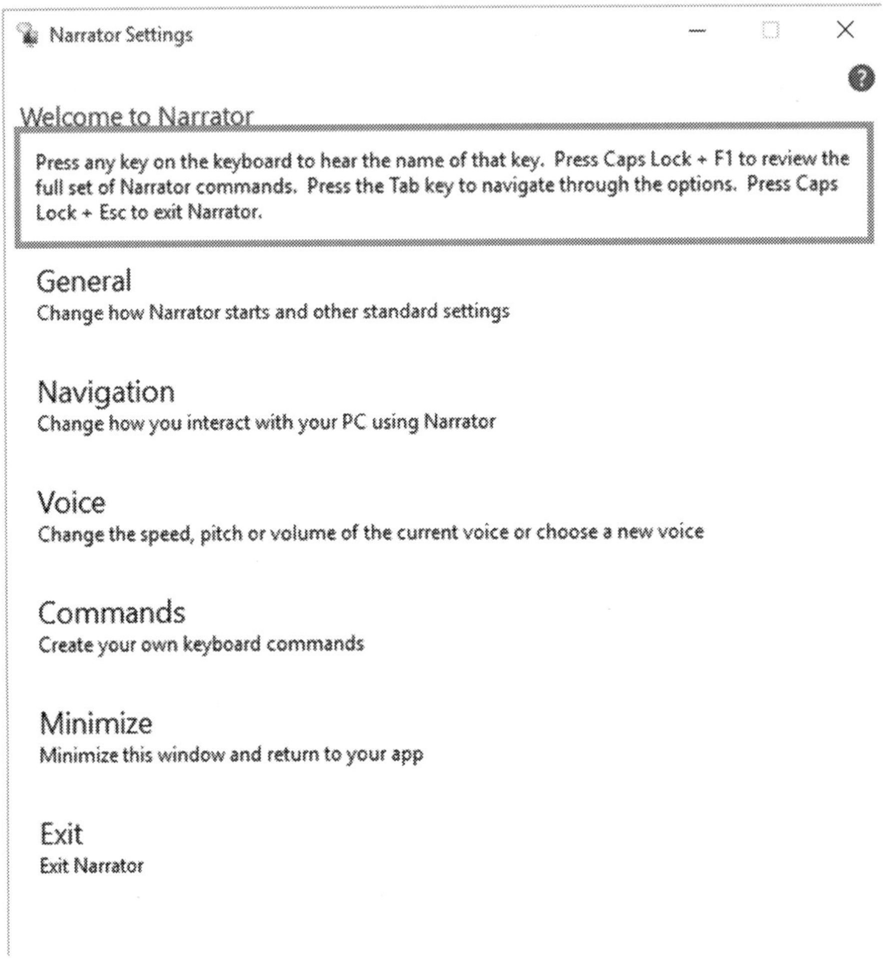

Narrator Settings   — ☐ ✕

❓

Welcome to Narrator

Press any key on the keyboard to hear the name of that key. Press Caps Lock + F1 to review the full set of Narrator commands. Press the Tab key to navigate through the options. Press Caps Lock + Esc to exit Narrator.

General
Change how Narrator starts and other standard settings

Navigation
Change how you interact with your PC using Narrator

Voice
Change the speed, pitch or volume of the current voice or choose a new voice

Commands
Create your own keyboard commands

Minimize
Minimize this window and return to your app

Exit
Exit Narrator

Figure 3-11. *The Narrator Settings dialog appears when you start the Narrator. It has these option categories, from top to bottom: General, Navigation, Voice, Commands, Minimize, and Exit*

General Settings

This is where you can find the main settings for the Narrator. They are presented as a series of check boxes with a drop-down menu below them (refer to Figure 3-12):

- *Lock The Narrator Key So You Don't Have To Press Them For Each Command (Caps Lock)*: When you activate commands in the Narrator, the Caps Lock key is very commonly used. This option allows you to lock Caps Lock on so you don't need to keep pressing it for each command you use. This option is not enabled by default

- *Hear Characters As You Type*: Reads individual characters as you type them on your physical or onscreen keyboard. This can help with typing accuracy. This option is enabled by default.

- *Hear Words As You Type*: Reads each complete word as you type it. This option is enabled by default.

- *Read Out Voiced Narrator Errors*: Reads errors encountered with the Narrator. This option is enabled by default.

- *Highlight Cursor*: Places a highlight box around your cursor onscreen to help you see it. This option is enabled by default.

- *Play Audio Cues*: Windows 10 can use sound to inform you of actions you perform and events that occur onscreen. This option is enabled by default. The following audio cues are used in the Narrator:

  - Moving to the next item plays a "tick."

  - Activating an item plays a "click."

  - Scrolling plays a sliding sound.

  - Selecting an item plays a "thud."

  - Narrator errors play a "bloop" sound.

  - When you navigate the screen with a single finger, the Narrator plays a "tick" for each new item you touch.

- *Read UI Hints And Tips*: Helps you navigate Windows 10 and your apps. This option is enabled by default.

- *Lower The Volume Of Other Apps When Narrator Is Running*: Helps you hear the Narrator better by reducing the volume of audio and other open apps. This option is enabled by default.

- *Retain Notifications To Be Read For*: A drop-down menu that keeps pop-up toast notifications for between 5 seconds and 10 minutes so that you can have them read by the Narrator.

There are Save Changes and Discard Changes buttons below these options.

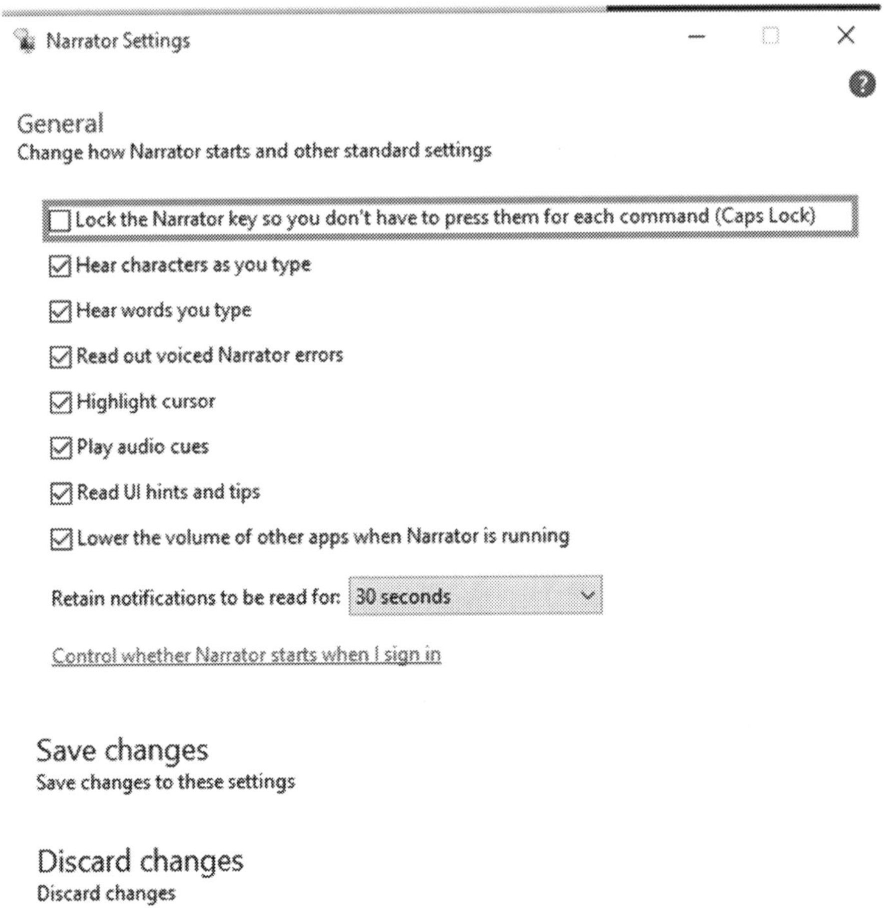

🐿 Narrator Settings   —   ☐   ✕

❓

General
Change how Narrator starts and other standard settings

☐ Lock the Narrator key so you don't have to press them for each command (Caps Lock)

☑ Hear characters as you type

☑ Hear words you type

☑ Read out voiced Narrator errors

☑ Highlight cursor

☑ Play audio cues

☑ Read UI hints and tips

☑ Lower the volume of other apps when Narrator is running

Retain notifications to be read for: [30 seconds   ⌄]

Control whether Narrator starts when I sign in

Save changes
Save changes to these settings

Discard changes
Discard changes

Figure 3-12. *The General Narrator Settings include options with check boxes to activate or deactivate each one. They are presented in a vertical list*

Navigation Settings

The Navigation settings help you choose how to interact with your PC using the Narrator (refer to Figure 3-13):

- *Read And Interact With The Screen Using The Mouse*: Not enabled by default, because the standard method of navigating the screen using the Narrator is to use the cursor and Tab keys on your keyboard to move around within the currently selected app. Two sub-options can change how you use the Narrator. These options are not enabled by default:

  - *Use The Numeric Keypad To Move The Mouse Around The Screen*: Changes the operation of the number pad on your keyboard (if you have one) so that the numbers 1 to 9 act as a mouse trackpad, moving the cursor. You can hold the Ctrl key to make the cursor jump more quickly in steps.

  - *Narrator Cursor Follows Mouse Cursor*: Always reads aloud the item currently underneath the mouse cursor.

- *Activate Keys On The Touch Keyboard When You Lift Your Finger*: Can make using the onscreen keyboard easier. When you turn on the Narrator, it reads aloud the key your finger is touching. The default action is that you then have to lift your finger and again tap the letter onscreen. This option selects the letter automatically when you lift your finger. This option is not enabled by default.

- *Narrator Cursor Follows Keyboard Focus*: As you use the cursor and Tab keys on your keyboard to move between items onscreen, the Narrator follows you. This option, which is enabled by default, allows you to turn this feature off if you would prefer the Narrator to just follow your mouse.

- *Enable The Text Insertion Point To Follow The Narrator Cursor*: This option is also enabled by default and can make it easier to type in apps and search boxes.

- *Select The Narrator Cursor Movement Mode*: A drop-down dialog with two options, Normal and Advanced. In Windows 8, Microsoft introduced new touch gestures to the Narrator including using finger left and right flicks to move through items onscreen. If you would prefer the Narrator to read every item on a page from top to bottom, choose the Advanced option.

Again, as with all the settings for the Narrator, there are Save Changes and Discard Changes buttons below these options.

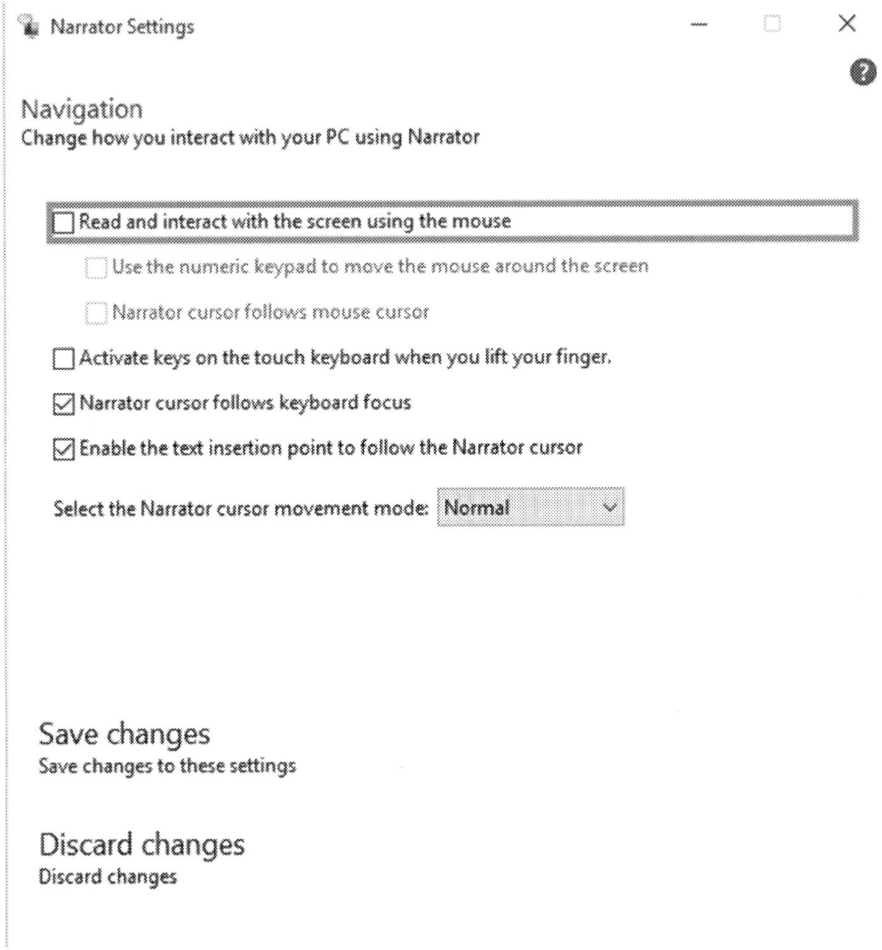

Figure 3-13. *The Navigation settings consist of check box options, aligned vertically with a drop-down option beneath them*

Voice Settings

The Voice settings let you choose how the Narrator communicates with you (refer to Figure 3-14):

- *Select The Speed Of The Voice*: Lets you slow down or speed up the Narrator voice. This is presented as a horizontal slider control.

- *Select The Volume Of The Voice*: Set to maximum by default and is a horizontal slider control.

- *Select The Pitch Of The Voice*: Allows you to dampen the voice or make it brighter. This is also presented as a horizontal slider control.

- *Select A Different Voice For The Narrator*: Lets you choose from different voices from a drop-down options box. The available voices may vary depending on your country and language.

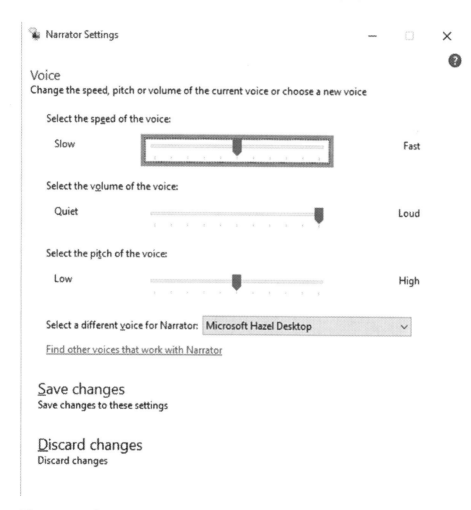

Figure 3-14. *The Voice settings are presented as three horizontal slider controls with a drop-down option box below them*

Command Settings

I mentioned earlier in this chapter that many of the commands you use in the Narrator require the use of the Caps Lock key. You can customize these commands if you wish in the Commands settings; refer to Figure 3-15.

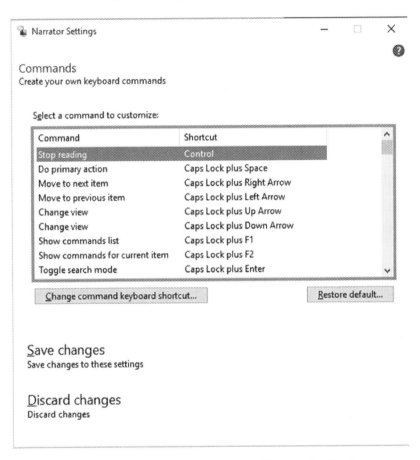

Figure 3-15. *The Narrator commands are presented in a vertical list. You can scroll down the list to select a command and then select the Change Command Keyboard Shortcut button below and to the left of the list. To the right of the Change Shortcut button is a Restore Default button*

Table 3-1 contains a complete list of the commands available in the Narrator, together with their keyboard shortcuts.

Table 3-1. *Narrator Keyboard Commands*

Command	Keyboard shortcut
Stop reading.	Ctrl
Start reading.	Caps Lock+M
Increase the voice volume.	Caps Lock+Page Up
Decrease the voice volume.	Caps Lock+Page Down
Increase the voice speed.	Caps Lock+Plus (+)
Decrease the voice speed.	Caps Lock+Minus (-)
Read the current date and time.	Caps Lock+C
Read the item.	Caps Lock+D
Read the item spelled out.	Caps Lock+S
Repeat the phrase.	Caps Lock+V
Read the window.	Caps Lock+W
Read the document.	Caps Lock+H
Read the current page.	Caps Lock+Ctrl+U
Read the next page.	Caps Lock+U
Read the previous page.	Caps Lock+Shift+U
Read the current paragraph.	Caps Lock+Ctrl+I
Read the next paragraph.	Caps Lock+I
Read the previous paragraph.	Caps Lock+Shift+I
Read the current time.	Caps Lock+Ctrl+O
Read the next line.	Caps Lock+O
Read the previous line.	Caps Lock+Shift+O
Read the current word.	Caps Lock+Ctrl+P
Read the next word.	Caps Lock+P
Read the previous word.	Caps Lock+Shift+P
Read all the items in containing area.	Caps Lock+R
Move to the last item in the containing area.	Caps Lock+Q
Move to the beginning of the text.	Caps Lock+Y
Move to the end of the text.	Caps Lock+B
Jump to the next heading.	Caps Lock+J
Jump to the previous heading.	Caps Lock+Shift+J

(*continued*)

Table 3-1. (*continued*)

Command	Keyboard shortcut
Jump to the next table.	Caps Lock+K
Jump to the previous table.	Caps Lock+Shift+K
Jump to the next link.	Caps Lock+L
Jump to the previous link.	Caps Lock+Shift+L
Jump to the next cell in the row.	Caps Lock+F3
Jump to the previous cell in the row.	Caps Lock+Shift+F3
Jump to the next cell in the column	Caps Lock+F4
Jump to the previous cell in the column.	Caps Lock+Shift+F4
Do the primary action.	Caps Lock+Space
Move to the next item.	Caps Lock+Right Arrow
Move to the previous item.	Caps Lock+Left Arrow
Change the view.	Caps Lock+Up/Down Arrow
Show the commands list.	Caps Lock+F1
Show the commands for the current item.	Caps Lock+F2
Toggle character reading.	Caps Lock+F12
Toggle search mode.	Caps Lock+Enter
Toggle mouse mode.	Caps Lock+Num Lock
Change the verbosity mode.	Caps Lock+A
Exit the Narrator.	Caps Lock+Esc
Lock the Narrator key (Caps Lock).	Caps Lock+Z
Move the Narrator cursor to the system cursor.	Caps Lock+G
Move the Narrator cursor to the pointer.	Caps Lock+T
Go back one item.	Caps Lock+Backspace
Jump to the linked item.	Caps Lock+Insert
Read the current column.	Caps Lock+F7
Read the current row.	Caps Lock+F8
Read the current column header.	Caps Lock+F9
Read the current row header.	Caps Lock+F10
Read which row and column the Narrator is in.	Caps Lock+F5
Jump to a table cell.	Caps Lock+F6
Jump to cell contents.	Caps Lock+Shift+F6
Navigate to the parent.	Caps Lock+Ctrl+Left Arrow
Navigate to the next sibling.	Caps Lock+Ctrl+Down Arrow
Navigate to the previous sibling.	Caps Lock+Ctrl+Up Arrow

Using the Narrator with Touch

You can also use the Narrator with touch on either a touchscreen or laptop trackpad. Many gestures are available to help make it easier to use your PC; refer to Table 3-2.

Table 3-2. *Narrator Touch Gestures*

Touch Gesture	Command
Tap or drag.	Read the item under your finger.
Double-tap *or* hold with one finger and tap anywhere with a second.	Do the primary action.
Triple-tap *or* hold with one finger and double-tap with a second.	Do the secondary action.
Flick left or right.	Move to the previous/next item.
Flick up or down.	Change the move increment.
Hold with one finger and two-finger-tap with additional fingers.	Start dragging or extra key options.
Two-finger tap.	Stop speaking.
Two-finger swipe.	Scroll.
Three-finger tap.	Show/hide the Narrator settings window.
Three-finger swipe up.	Read the current window.
Three-finger swipe down.	Read from the current location in text.
Three-finger swipe left or right.	TAB forward and backward.
Four-finger tap.	Show the commands for current item.
Four-finger double tap.	Toggle search mode.
Four-finger triple tap.	Show the Narrator commands list.
Four-finger swipe up or down.	Enable/disable semantic zoom (semantic zoom provides a high-level view of large blocks of content).

Additional Narrator Settings

Back in the Settings app, some of the main Narrator controls are available as toggle switches or sliders (refer to Figure 3-16):

- *Start Narrator Automatically*: Turns on the Narrator whenever you sign in to your PC. This toggle switch is not enabled by default when you turn on the Narrator.

- *Voice*: Allows you to choose a voice for the narrator from a drop-down box.

- *Speed/Pitch*: Two horizontal sliders for controlling the Narrator voice.

- *Sounds You Hear*: Contains five check boxes:

  - Read Hints For Controls And Buttons

  - Characters You Type

  - Words You Type

  - Lower The Volume Of Other Applications When Narrator Is Running

  - Play Audio Cues

- *Cursor And Keys*: Contains three sub-options to help you use your cursor with the Narrator:

  - Highlight The Cursor

  - Have Insertion Point Follow Narrator

  - Activate Keys On Touch Keyboard When I Lift My Finger Off The Keyboard

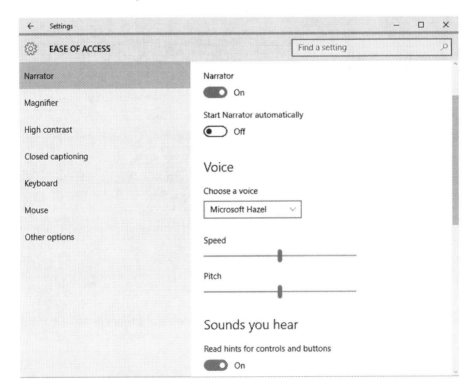

Figure 3-16. *Some of the main Narrator controls are available in the Settings app*

Using Windows 10's Tools to Highlight Activities Onscreen

The Magnifier, high-contrast themes, and the Narrator are fantastic tools for making it easier to see (and hear) what's on your screen. Visually impaired PC users may also face the challenge of finding the right controls to use onscreen or on your keyboard.

This can make it difficult to focus on what you're doing and hamper your productivity. It's not helpful when your focus is distracted because you're searching for the right button or key to press, or because you can't see or hear notifications from apps that may be directly relevant to what you're doing at the time.

This isn't restricted to people with visual, hearing, or cogitative difficulties. People who work in noisy or distracting environments can also benefit from Windows 10's tools that make it easier to see and understand what's going on on your desktop.

In Chapter 6, I show you to make it much easier to focus on tasks and how to make yourself more productive in Windows 10.

Summary

There are plenty of ways both to interact with your PC and to have your PC interact with you. You may even want to use some of these Ease of Access tools in conjunction with one another, perhaps using both the Narrator and Speech Recognition, or a high-contrast theme and the Magnifier. Microsoft has put considerable thought and effort into making PC use straightforward for people who have trouble seeing their screen, and these tools are indeed very powerful and flexible.

■ ■ ■

CHAPTER 4

Creating Visual Alternatives for Sound

Although a screen is and will always be the main interface we use for PCs, sound plays an important part as well. If you sit in a bar or café for any length of time, you hear various notification sounds around you coming from smartphones, laptops, and tablets. Each one informs the owner of the device about something important: a message, an e-mail, a security alert, or perhaps that an update is available for an app.

Sometimes, PC sounds are crucial. We increasingly use devices to watch video at home and on the move. But if you have difficulty hearing your PC, what can you do? Turning up the volume to a level at which you can hear notifications will likely annoy the people around you, and headphones may be bulky or impractical. This chapter shows you the ways in which you can use visual alternatives for sound on your PC.

Replacing Audible Alerts with Visual Alerts

There are many scenarios in which you may find it difficult to hear or easy to miss audible alerts on your PC. You may be in a café or bar, as I mentioned earlier, or in a meeting or a college lecture, or working in a busy or noisy environment, or just want some peace and quiet.

You may have your smartphone set to vibrate, to discretely alert you that something wants your attention. But you can't set your PC, laptop, or tablet to vibrate.

The Other Options section of the Ease of Access settings includes an option to use Visual Notifications For Sound; refer to Figure 4-1.

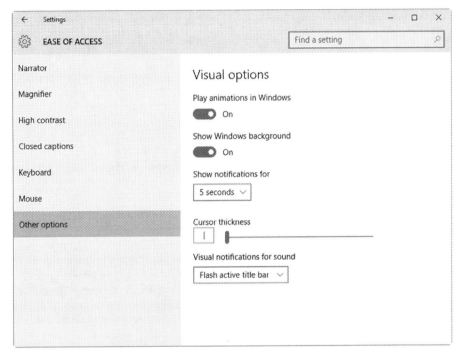

Figure 4-1. You can activate a Visual Notifications For Sound feature in the Ease of Access Other options. It is a drop-down menu at the bottom of the list

The first option here is Flash Active Title Bar, which flashes the bar across the top of the window that seeks your attention. This is the most subtle effect and may be easy to miss.

Flash Active Window flashes the entire window that seeks your attention. This is more visible, unless that window is hidden or minimized.

Flash Entire Display is what I call "shouty mode." The entire screen flashes for a second to alert you that a notification has arrived, although you then have to go and hunt for it.

It's worth noting at this point that notifications that do not directly apply to an app but that appear anyway, such as app and Windows Update notifications, always flash the window you're currently using.

Adding Closed Captioning to Video

Video subtitles can be incredibly useful if you have difficulty hearing dialogue in a television program or movie. Subtitles also come in handy if you want to watch a video but don't want to wake somebody else up, or if you're learning a foreign language and want to listen to the words and see the translation live onscreen.

All editions of Windows 10 support closed captioning, but only for compatible apps. These include the Movies & TV app that comes with Windows 10; check the details for other apps before you purchase them, to see if they are compatible with Windows 10's closed-captioning system.

You can find Closed Captions as an option in the Ease of Access settings; refer to Figure 4-2.

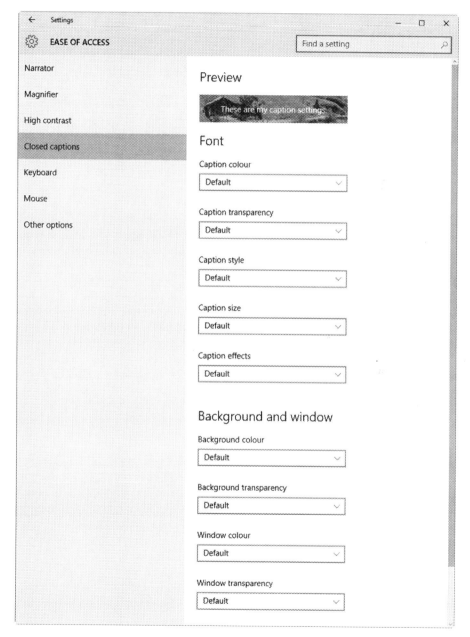

Figure 4-2. *The closed-captioning options are available in all editions of Windows 10 and on every Windows 10 device, including smartphones*

At the top of the closed-captioning options is a display showing you how your captions will look when played over a video. You can change how the captions' appearance using various options.

The Font options allow you to choose a typeface that is easy and clear to read. Additionally, you can choose the text color, transparency, size, and effects, such as a drop shadow.

You can also choose options for the background. If you find subtitles difficult to read on some video, especially those with lighter pictures, you can change the background color to black and the transparency to opaque. Doing so adds a black box in which the subtitles appear.

Playing Closed-Captioned Video in the Movies & TV App

You can purchase or rent videos in the Windows Store app and through the Movies & TV app in Windows 10. When you are deciding what to purchase, look for the Closed Captioning icon (refer to Figure 4-3) to see whether subtitles are provided for the video.

Figure 4-3. *The Closed Captioning icon is shown if subtitles are provided when you purchase or rent a video*

Once you have a video in your library that includes subtitles, a CC icon appears with the controls when you play the video in the Windows 10 Movies & TV app; refer to Figure 4-4.

Figure 4-4. *You can turn on subtitles in the Movies & TV app by selecting the CC button*

Activating Subtitles for YouTube Videos

If, like a lot of people, you enjoy watching videos on the YouTube web site, you'll be pleased to know that subtitling is available on a great many videos. Some of this is added by video producers, and the rest is added automatically by YouTube's system, although this latter option is less accurate.

Videos that have closed-captioning support feature the CC icon next to their details. When you are playing a video in YouTube, click the Settings (cog) icon in the play controls, and Subtitles appears as one of the options; refer to Figure 4-5.

Figure 4-5. *You can activate subtitles in YouTube videos by selecting the Settings icon to the right of the play controls*

Selecting this option lets you choose between the provided subtitles (if available) and autogenerated subtitles, and to activate auto-translation if the video is not in your language. Additionally, just as with the closed-captioning options in Windows 10, you can choose the font, color, and opacity of the text and background.

Summary

Being able to use visual alternatives for sound offers many benefits, and these are not restricted to people who have difficulty hearing their PCs. For example, you may be in a busy or noisy environment, working in a library where quiet is enforced, or learning a foreign language. Whatever your needs, Windows 10 can alert you to notifications and provide subtitles for video both on your PC and through services such as YouTube, with quick and easy-to-use controls.

CHAPTER 5

▦ ▦ ▦

Making the Mouse and Keyboard Easier to Use

What use is a desktop PC, laptop, or convertible tablet, such as the Microsoft Surface, if you can't get the stuff done on the desktop that you need to, using the apps that you want to use? Productivity is everything with PCs, whether it's working, gaming, or using the Internet for shopping, banking, or keeping up with friends and family. We need all of our apps and our copy of Windows to work with us, not against us.

It's here that Windows 10 and your apps may surprise you. There are features designed for all users of PCs that can prove extremely useful in making things more accessible for you, and if this doesn't prove that accessibility can be appropriate for almost anybody, I'm not sure what will.

Making Your Keyboard Easy to Use

We tend to think of think of printers being the most commonly used peripheral with PCs, but actually keyboards and mice are the most commonly used. They're technically part of the PC, at least insofar as a desktop or laptop cannot be used without them (or a trackpad, in the case of a laptop), but peripherals they are, and essential they certainly are.

This doesn't mean keyboards and mice are easy to use. A large ecosystem of accessible peripherals exists. These include keyboards with oversized keys and/or text, mice with large buttons, and handle-style paddle mice that can easily be gripped and moved with one hand. You may have seen or used these peripherals yourself, and they are sometimes seen on the desks of people who have suffered repetitive strain injury (RSI).

You don't need to spend money, which you may not even have available, to make your keyboard or mouse easier to use. Windows 10 includes tools to help with this, and they're very extensive.

The Onscreen Keyboards

In the Ease of Access settings, in the Settings app (you spend a lot of time with these throughout this book, so from here I'll just refer to them as the Ease of Access settings) is a category for Keyboard settings; refer to Figure 5-1.

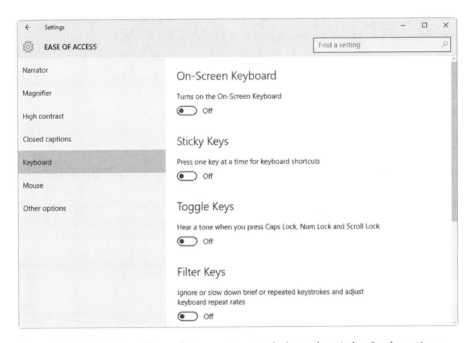

Figure 5-1. *The Keyboard Ease of Access settings include toggle switches for the options to display the onscreen keyboard, use Sticky Keys, Toggle Keys, and Filter Keys, with other settings at the bottom of the list*

Each option in the Keyboard section is a toggle key with a simple on/off setting. On-Screen Keyboard (refer to Figure 5-2) is the first option: this displays a keyboard on your screen that floats on the desktop and that can be used with all your apps.

Figure 5-2. *The onscreen keyboard is a full PC keyboard that can float on your desktop*

But how is the onscreen keyboard different from Windows 10's onscreen keyboard, you ask? This is a very interesting and important question, because the onscreen keyboard is completely different than the onscreen keyboard, and I wouldn't want you to be confused.

If you use a tablet or a laptop or desktop that has a touchscreen, then when you tap with your finger in a text-entry field in an app or a Windows feature, the onscreen keyboard appears; refer to Figure 5-3.

Figure 5-3. *The touchscreen keyboard appears when you tap a text-input area on a touchscreen PC*

This onscreen keyboard has three controls in its top-right corner:

- *Undock*: An icon you can grab lets you move the keyboard around the screen.

- *Maximize*: Expands the keyboard so that it fills the bottom portion of your screen. All running apps are automatically resized to occupy only the remaining space, so that the keyboard does not overlap them.

- *Close*: Hides the keyboard.

There are some advantages to using this keyboard. It's easily accessed because an icon to open it appears at far right on your desktop Taskbar, just to the left of the clock. If you do not see the icon, perhaps because you don't have a touchscreen, you can enable its view by right-clicking (or touching and holding) the Taskbar and selecting Show Touch Keyboard Button in the options menu that appears.

This onscreen keyboard can be of most use if you need to use the extended character set, which includes international letters and symbols. Selecting and holding a key displays international variations on that letter that you can select; refer to Figure 5-4.

Figure 5-4. *Selecting and holding a letter, number, or symbol on the Windows 10 onscreen keyboard can display additional characters that you can select*

This also works in Symbol and Number mode. Select this by selecting the &123 button at bottom-left on the keyboard; it can display numbers in subscript and superscript, as well as variations on symbols.

In the bottom-right corner of the onscreen keyboard is an Options button. Select this, and a pop-up menu of different keyboard layouts appears; refer to Figure 5-5. These options are as follows, from left to right:

- *Standard onscreen keyboard*: Displays letters, and numbers and symbols are available on a button in the bottom-left corner

- *Thumb keyboard*: Splits the keys between the left and right sides of your screen, enabling use with your thumbs on a tablet PC

- *Handwriting*: Removes the keyboard and replaces it with a panel you can write in with a stylus or your finger

- *Full keyboard*: Grayed out and unavailable by default but can be switched on for touchscreen devices. In the Settings app, go to Devices and then Typing and activate the option Add The Standard Keyboard Layout As A Touch Keyboard Option.

Figure 5-5. *The Options button in the bottom-right corner of the onscreen keyboard presents a pop-up of different keyboard options, including standard, thumb keyboard, and handwriting*

▓ **Tip**   To add the full keyboard option to non-touchscreen devices, you need to use the Registry Editor. Search for Regedit on the Start menu or in Cortana. This should always be done with extreme care, and you should choose Export from the File menu to make a backup copy of the Registry first.

Navigate in the Registry Editor to `HKEY_LOCAL_MACHINE\SOFTWARE\Microsoft\` `TabletTip\1.7`. In an empty area in the right pane, right-click (or touch and hold), create a new `DWORD` called `EnableCompatibilityKeyboard`, and give it a value of 1.

Let's get back to the Ease of Access onscreen keyboard you saw way back in Figure 5-2 (don't worry—I'll show it again shortly). This is different from the onscreen keyboard that ships in Windows 10 for touchscreen devices, because it includes additional accessibility options.

The Ease of Access onscreen keyboard is also a full PC keyboard and includes keys such as Function (Fn), Control (Ctrl), Print Screen (PrtScn), Page up (PgUp), Page Down (PgDn), Home and End. The PC's function keys (F1 to F12) are available by pressing the Fn key in the bottom-left corner of the keyboard, should you need these for use in your apps. Selecting AltGr to the right of the spacebar displays some international characters and symbols; refer to Figure 5-6.

Figure 5-6. *Selecting the AltGr button to the right of the spacebar on the onscreen keyboard displays some international characters and symbols*

Selecting the Options button at lower right on the keyboard displays a window with additional controls for the keyboard; refer to Figure 5-7. These options are as follows:

- *Use Click Sound*: Enables or disables an audible click through your PCs speakers when a key is pressed.

- *Show Keys To Make It Easier To Move Around The Screen*: Enables or disables the Nav, Move Up, Move Down, Dock, and Fade buttons at far right on the keyboard.

- *Turn On Numeric Key Pad*: Displays a numeric pad to the right of the keyboard.

- *Click On Keys / Hover Over Keys*: Enable the use of the keyboard without having to click the keys with a mouse or your finger. You can choose how long to hover your mouse over the key for it to be selected.

- *Scan Through Keys*: Allows you to use one key on your keyboard (the spacebar is set by default) to select the key you want. Each row of keys is highlighted, one after the other. When the row containing the key you want is highlighted, press Space, and then selections of keys will be highlighted on that row. When the selection gets to the key you want, click Space again, and the highlight cycles between specific keys so you can select the one you wish to use.

- *Text Prediction*: A feature you may be familiar with on smartphones that lets Windows 10 predict what you're likely to want to type next, based on the words already typed. Predicted words appear above the onscreen keyboard and can be clicked or tapped to select them. Text prediction is excellent in Windows 10, and entire sentences can be completed using it.

Figure 5-7. *The onscreen keyboard Options button displays a dialog with options to use click sounds, show a numeric pad, and more*

Unlike the Windows 10 touchscreen keyboard that I described earlier, the Ease of Access keyboard floats in a window that be moved and resized to suit your individual needs. If, for example, you need the keyboard to be larger, you select and drag one of its corners to make it larger. As I have detailed, it's also much more powerful and flexible than the standard onscreen keyboard. It's able to display more keys and is far more accessible.

Sticky Keys

If you find it difficult to use two- or three-keypress combinations, such as Ctrl+C (Copy), Ctrl+V (Paste), and Ctrl+Alt+Del (it's all gone horribly wrong), the Sticky Keys option is the solution; refer to Figure 5-8.

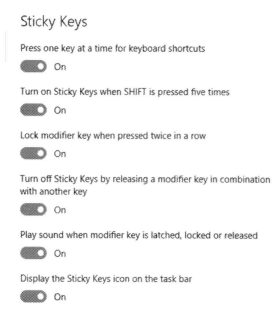

Figure 5-8. *Sticky Keys is a toggle switch than can make two- and three-keypress combinations easier*

With Sticky Keys enabled, you can press just one key at a time and still use two- and three-key combinations. For example, you can press the Ctrl key and then release it, and Windows will give you some time to then press another key, such as X (Cut).

Additional options are available, each as a toggle switch below the main Sticky Keys option. These expand to display in the Settings app when Sticky Keys is enabled:

- Press one key at a time for keyboard shortcuts.

- Turn on Sticky Keys when Shift is pressed five times.

- Lock modifier key when pressed twice in a row (the modifier keys are Shift, Ctrl, and Alt).

- Turn off Sticky Keys by releasing a modifier key in combination with another key.

- Play sound when modifier key is latched, locked, or released.

- Display the Sticky Keys icon on the Taskbar.

▩ **Tip**   You can also turn on Sticky Keys by repeatedly pressing one of the Shift keys on your keyboard. This displays an option dialog asking if you want to turn on the feature; refer to Figure 5-9.

Figure 5-9. *You can also turn on Sticky Keys by repeatedly pressing the Shift key on your keyboard*

Toggle Keys

If you're really angry, you might want to type at somebody ENTIRELY IN CAPITAL LETTERS!!! But otherwise, it can be really annoying to discover that you've enabled or disabled Caps Lock or Num Lock accidentally—and let's face it, we've *all* done this.

The Toggle Keys option plays a tone through your PC's speakers when you press the Caps Lock, Num Lock, or Scroll Lock key; refer to Figure 5-10.

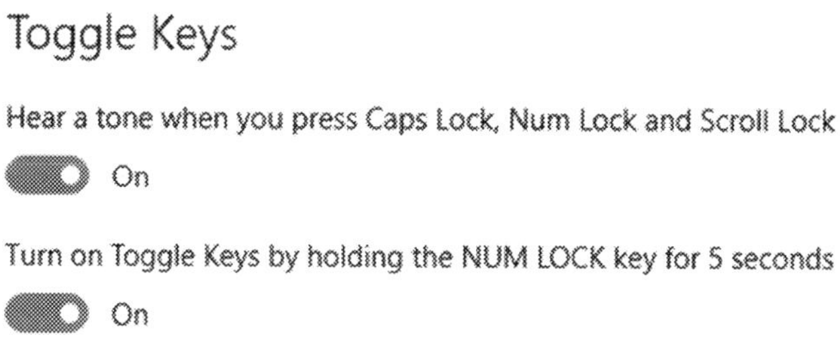

Toggle Keys

Hear a tone when you press Caps Lock, Num Lock and Scroll Lock

⬤▭◯ On

Turn on Toggle Keys by holding the NUM LOCK key for 5 seconds

⬤▭◯ On

Figure 5-10. *Activating Toggle Keys presents an option to turn the feature on and off by pressing the Num Lock key five times*

Filter Keys

Filter Keys makes it generally easier to use your keyboard. There are various options available; refer to Figure 5-11.

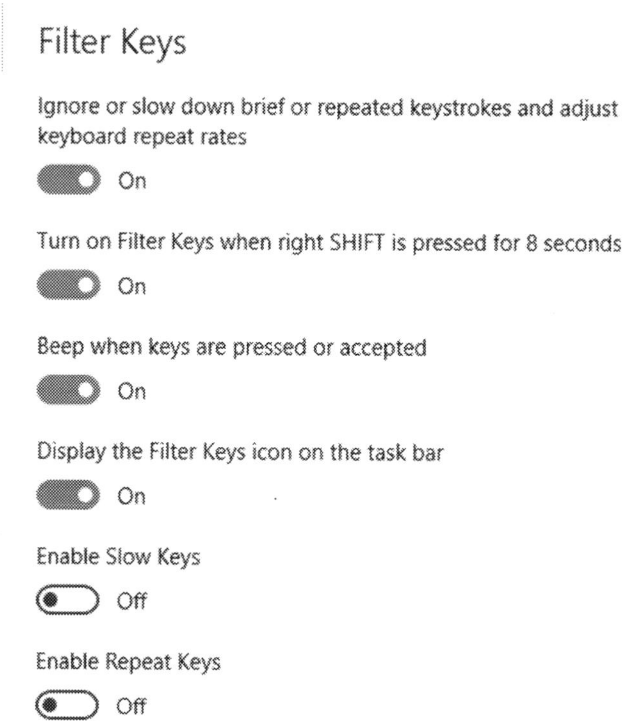

Filter Keys

Ignore or slow down brief or repeated keystrokes and adjust keyboard repeat rates

⬤▭◯ On

Turn on Filter Keys when right SHIFT is pressed for 8 seconds

⬤▭◯ On

Beep when keys are pressed or accepted

⬤▭◯ On

Display the Filter Keys icon on the task bar

⬤▭◯ On

Enable Slow Keys

◯⬤▭ Off

Enable Repeat Keys

◯⬤▭ Off

Figure 5-11. *Filter Keys makes it generally easier to use your keyboard*

When Filter Keys is switched on, the following sub-options become available:

- *Ignore Or Slow Down Brief Or Repeated Keystrokes And Adjust Keyboard Rates*: This can be extremely helpful if your finger tends to sit on keys too long and automatically trigger the auto-repeat function, so that instead of typing **f**, you end up with **ffffff**.

- *Turn On Filter Keys When Right SHIFT Is Pressed For 8 Seconds*: This is self-explanatory.

- *Beep When Keys Are Pressed Or Accepted*: This makes a cool click sound that might remind you of the home computer you had when you were young.

- *Display The Filter Keys Icon On The Taskbar*: Again, this is self-explanatory.

- *Enable Slow Keys*: This is extremely useful if you often hit an incorrect key. With Slow Keys enabled, you have to press and hold a key for a period (by default, 1 second) for it to register as a keypress.

- *Enable Repeat Keys*: This is another useful feature if you find that you press keys for too long, and the repeated-key function starts. Here you can choose how long you need to hold the key—from 0.3 to 2 seconds—before auto-repeat begins.

Other Keyboard Settings

At the bottom of the Keyboard Ease of Access options are some settings that don't fall into any of the main categories I've already detailed (refer to Figure 5-12):

- *Enable Shortcut Underlines*: Underlines any links and shortcuts in Windows 10. Normally these shortcuts are highlighted in a different color, and this option makes it easier to see that they are selectable.

- *Display A Warning Message/Make A Sound When Turning A Setting On With A Shortcut*: Alerts you visually or audibly if you turn on an Ease of Access feature through a keyboard press, such as pressing or holding the Shift key.

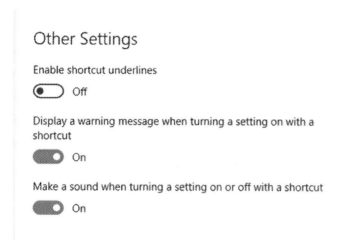

Figure 5-12. *At the bottom of the keyboard, Ease of Access options and toggle switches let you enable shortcut underlines, display a warning message when turning a setting on with a shortcut, and make a sound when turning a setting on or off with a shortcut*

Making Your Mouse Easier to Use

Fewer options are available to make your mouse easier to use than are available for your keyboard. This is because the mouse is a much simpler and more straightforward input device; refer to Figure 5-13.

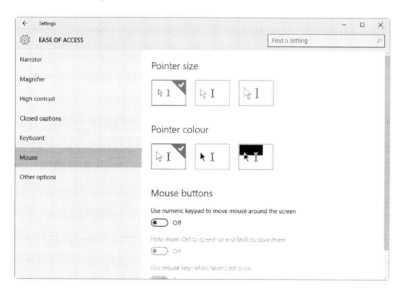

Figure 5-13. *Ease of Access options for the mouse allow you to change the pointer size and color, and control the mouse with the cursor keys on your keyboard*

At the top of the Mouse Ease of Access options are six boxes aligned in two rows:

- The top row presents three different *Pointer Size* options, from standard on the left to extra-large on the right.

- The next row presents three *Pointer Color* options. These include, from left to right, white, black, and inverse (the mouse cursor changes from black to white to present the best contrast all the time).

- *Use Numeric Keypad To Move Mouse Around The Screen*: Allows you to use the up, down, left, and right keys on your keyboard or onscreen keyboard to move the mouse pointer.

- *Hold Down Ctrl To Speed Up And Shift To Slow Down*: Lets you change the speed at which the mouse pointer moves, when controlled through the keyboard cursor keys.

- *Use Mouse Keys When Num Lock Is On*: Allows you to use the/ (right slash), * (multiply), and – (minus) keys on your keyboard's numeric pad as the left, middle, and right mouse buttons.

Additional Keyboard and Mouse Settings in the Control Panel

I want to try wherever possible in this book to focus on using the Ease of Access controls in the Settings app—not just because they're the easiest and, if you'll excuse the pun, the most accessible to use, but also because almost everything you need is available there. Some additional Controls can be found in the Ease of Access Center in the Control Panel, and I showed you where to find this in Chapter 1.

Selecting Make The Keyboard Easier To Use presents a few useful additional options, such as Prevent Windows From Being Automatically Rearranged When Moved To The Edge Of The Screen; refer to Figure 5-14.

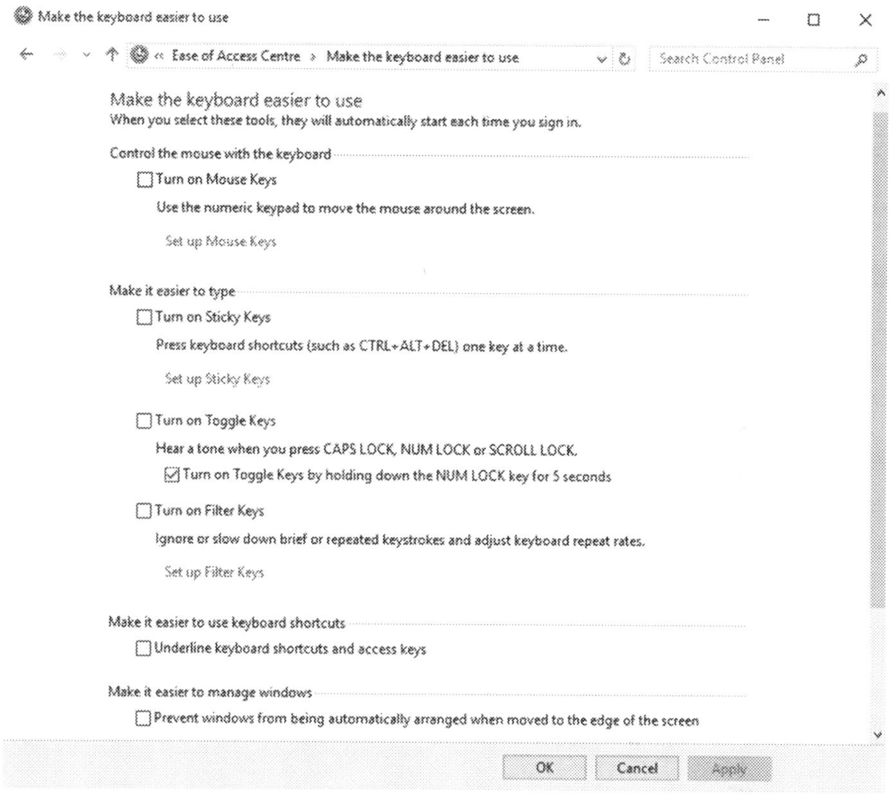

Figure 5-14. *Additional keyboard options are available in the Control Panel*

This disables the Snap feature in Windows 10 that you can use to have apps fill exactly 50% (both halves) or 25% (corners) of the screen when you drag them to an edge or corner. This can be handy if you find a mouse difficult to use.

Selecting the Make The Mouse Easier To Use link also presents additional options. You can select Set Up Mouse Keys (refer to Figure 5-15) for more control over using your keyboard to control the mouse pointer.

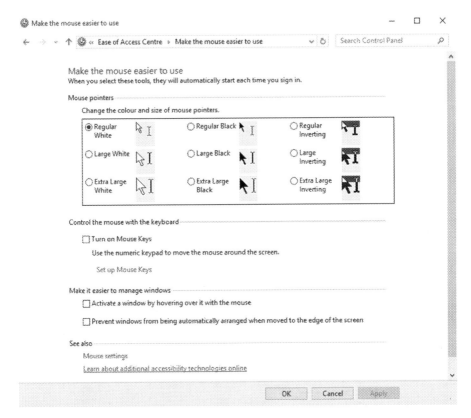

Figure 5-15. *You can get more control over using your keyboard to move the mouse pointer by selecting Set Up Mouse Keys in the Make The Mouse Easier To Use section in the Control Panel*

▓ **Tip**   When you grab a window and shake your mouse cursor in Windows 10, all other open windows on your desktop are minimized and hidden. Shake the window again, and all previously hidden windows reappear. You may find, however, that you're unsteady using a mouse, and you hide open windows when you don't want to. You can disable this feature by selecting the Prevent Windows From Being Automatically Arranged When Moved To The Edge Of The Screen option and then selecting the Apply button.

Sliders appear, which you can use to more finely control the speed of the mouse cursor and how it accelerates when you keep a cursor key pressed; refer to Figure 5-16.

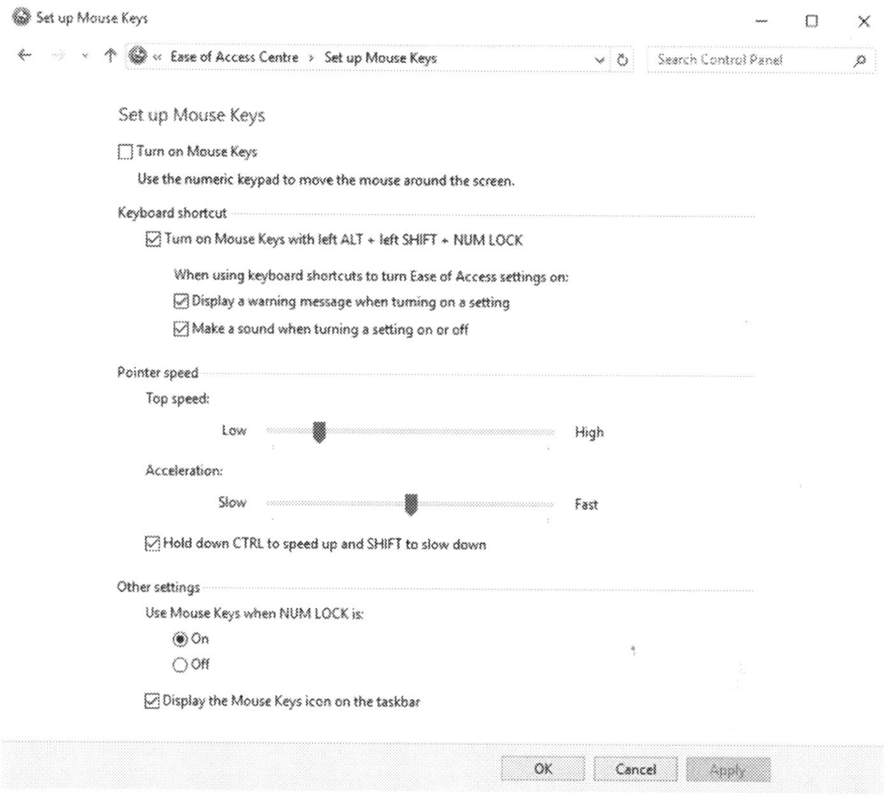

Figure 5-16. *You can finely control the speed and acceleration of mouse keys in the Control Panel using sliders*

Also from the Make The Mouse Easier To Use panel, you can select the Mouse Settings link. This displays a pop-up menu with additional controls and five tabs across the top; refer to Figure 5-17:

- *Buttons*: Contains the controls you need if you are left-handed of have trouble using the mouse buttons. You can switch he primary and secondary buttons and turn on ClickLock. You can also change the speed at which the double-click works, which can be useful if you are slow when using a mouse.

- ClickLock is a feature that allows you to drag and highlight windows, text, and areas onscreen without having to hold down the mouse button the whole time. When it is activated, select the item you want to drag or the beginning of the area you wish to highlight, and then release the button. Select again when you have moved the mouse to the correct area to place the window, or select items onscreen.

- *Pointers*: Lets you select different mouse-pointer schemes. Windows 10 includes 12 by default, and third-party themes can also be added through desktop theme packs.

- *Pointer Options*: Lets you change the speed at which the mouse moves and activate useful features such as making the mouse auto-snap to the closest window, displaying a trail to make it easy to follow the mouse onscreen, and highlighting the mouse pointer onscreen when you hold the Ctrl key.

- *Wheel*: Allows you to choose the speed at which vertical and, if supported by your mouse, horizontal scrolling work.

- *Hardware*: Contains technical hardware information about your mouse.

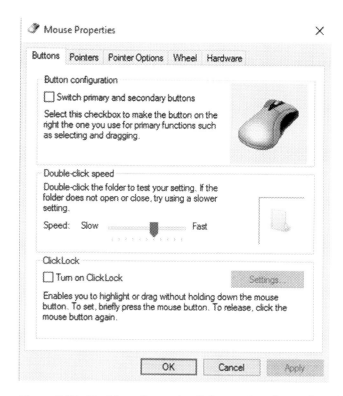

Figure 5-17. *The Mouse Properties dialog consists of controls on five tabs along the top of the window: Buttons, Pointers, Pointer Options, Wheel, and Hardware*

Summary

Given that the keyboard and mouse are the primary way to interact with PCs, it's unsurprising that this is where the most configuration options are to be found, and they are indeed extensive. Some options, however, can help any type of Windows user, from disabling auto-minimizing of open apps when you grab a window and shake the mouse cursor, to having Windows make an audible noise when you toggle Caps Lock and Num Lock on or off. Even if you don't find a keyboard or mouse difficult to use, you may still find some of these settings extremely convenient.

CHAPTER 6

Windows 10 for Memory, Learning, or Other Cognitive Impairments

If you find it difficult to concentrate on what you're doing on your PC, perhaps because you have a memory, learning, or other cognitive impairment, or perhaps just because you work in a busy or noisy environment, getting what you need done on your PC can be slow going.

Even factory workers can find it difficult to concentrate and focus on the task at hand. If you have difficulty focusing your concentration, then it's all too easy to miss an important alert or notification or to become distracted and lose your train of thought. Microsoft has thought about this and created some useful tools that can make it much easier to focus on whatever you need to do, no matter who you are, what you're doing, or where you are.

Making It Easier to Focus on Your Apps

When you're using a Windows 10 PC, laptop, or tablet, you can often find yourself with many apps and windows open on your screen, creating a confusing maelstrom of colors, shapes, text, and graphics. If you find it difficult to concentrate on work when this happens, there are some options available to you; refer to Figure 6-1.

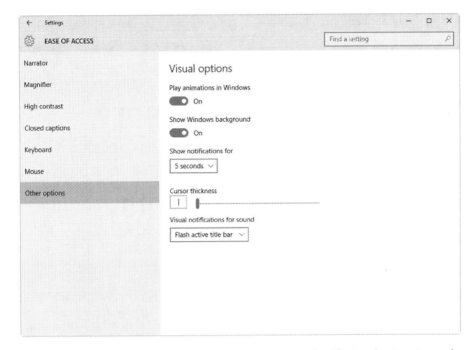

Figure 6-1. *Other Options in the Ease of Access settings can disable visual animation and your desktop wallpaper*

In the Ease of Access settings, select Other Options to find some useful tools to help you concentrate:

- *Play Animations In Windows*: Can disable all the visual animations on your PC, such as those that happen when apps open, close, or are minimized.

- *Show Windows Background*: Can hide your desktop wallpaper picture, replacing it with a plain black screen.

▓ **Tip**   On a smartphone, laptop, or tablet with an LED screen, black pixels do not draw any power, so having a plain black background can extend the battery life of your device.

- *Show Notifications For*: Extremely useful if the toast notifications in Windows (so called because they pop up) disappear from your desktop before you can read them. You can change the setting from 5 seconds to 5 minutes. Each toast can be manually dismissed by activating the close (X) button in its top-right corner.

- *Cursor Thickness*: Can change the thickness of your input cursor in apps such as e-mail and Microsoft Office, making it easier to see where the cursor is currently located.

- *Visual Notifications For Sound*: Can flash the title bar of an app, the entire app, or the entire desktop to alert you to a notification that is normally signaled through a sound. This can also be useful if you work in a very noisy environment.

Using Cortana as a PC Assistant

Microsoft introduced a new personal assistant called Cortana with Windows 10, and she (I prefer *she* to *it*) has some brilliant tricks up her sleeve to help anybody become more productive on their PC, laptop, tablet, or smartphone. If you have a visual impairment of any type and find it difficult to read things on your screen, Cortana can make your life considerably simpler, and you can have a pleasant conversation at the same time.

Cortana can remind you of events and appointments, track flights and packages, search for and aggregate documents, open apps on your PC, and even sing, tell you jokes, and speak Klingon. You need to activate Cortana before she'll do any of this, however. You can find her by clicking or tabbing to the Search box next to the Windows button on the far left of the Taskbar; refer to Figure 6-2.

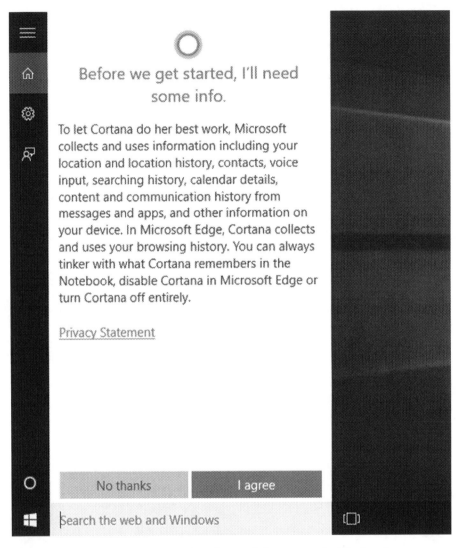

Figure 6-2. When you first click or tab to the search box next to the Windows button on the far left of the Taskbar at the bottom of your screen, you are asked if you want to set up Cortana

The process of setting up Cortana involves giving her some permissions, such as letting her know a little about you and your PC. Then, whenever you click or tab to the search box in the future, Cortana will appear instead of the basic Windows 10 file and Internet search feature.

You control Cortana by selecting the Notebook icon at top left in Cortana's windows and then selecting the Settings icon, which is shaped like a cog (although I still maintain it looks more like an English Rose); refer to Figure 6-3.

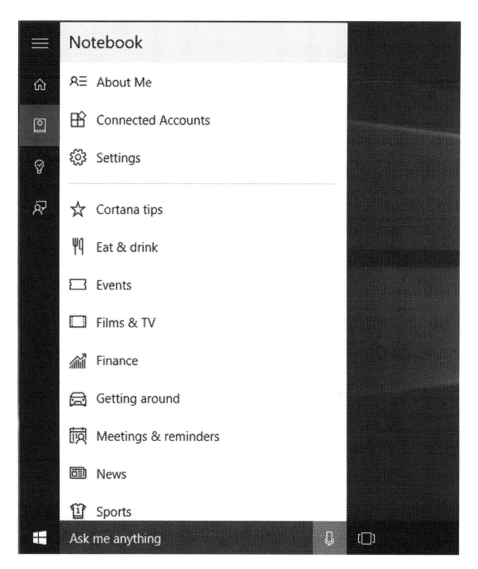

Figure 6-3. *You can control Cortana from her notebook. Options include (from top to bottom) About Me, where you can change your name and favorite places such as Home and Work; Connected Accounts, where you can set up additional work accounts that can sync with Cortana; and Settings*

When in Cortana's settings, you can activate the option to Let Cortana Respond To "Hey Cortana." If you have a microphone attached to your PC (they're built into almost every laptop and tablet and are in every smartphone), you can activate Cortana and control her with just your voice. Activating this displays a dialog in which your PC asks you to speak a phrase aloud, so it can learn your voice.

Below the Hey Cortana option is a setting to allow Cortana to respond to anyone or just yourself. If you are using a PC in a work environment, it's best to set Cortana to only respond to *your* voice and not to the joker who enjoys shouting "Hey Cortana" every time they walk past your desk; refer to Figure 6-4.

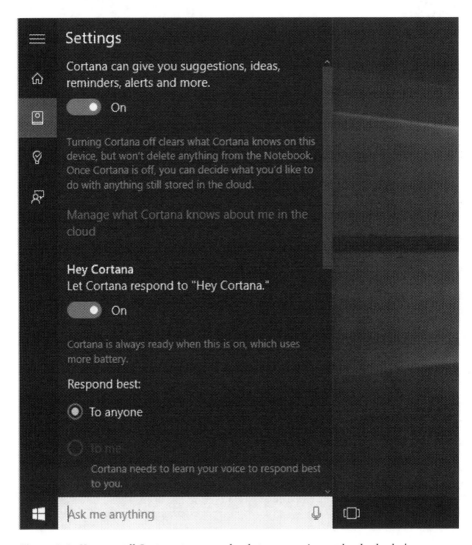

Figure 6-4. You can tell Cortana to respond only to your voice, and nobody else's

Other settings are available for Cortana, and Microsoft will expand her functionality over time to include more features. It's worth spending some time looking through the various options available for Cortana and telling her about the things you like or are most interested in. That way, when you open Cortana, she can also give you relevant information about news, sports, and weather without the need for you to open a separate app; refer to Figure 6-5.

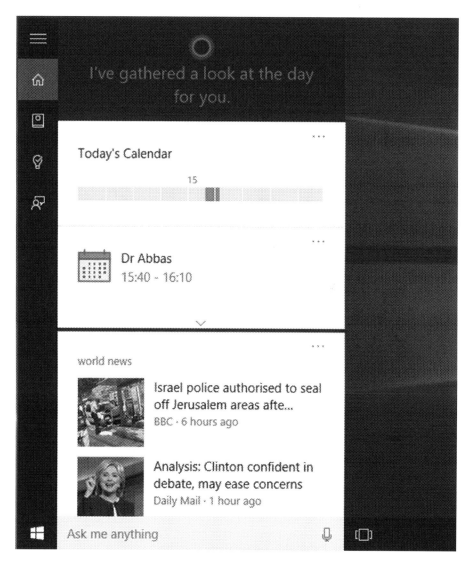

Figure 6-5. Cortana can show you your appointments, news, sports, weather, and more in her window when you click or tab into her search box

Summary

Having the ability to flash or highlight windows on the desktop and change the length of time that pop-up toast notifications appear are small changes that can make a huge difference in how productive you can be and help you focus on what you're doing. Using Cortana to provide useful and relevant formation for you can also minimize the amount of time you are away from your primary task. In Chapter 9, I'll show you some tips and tricks you can use with Cortana to set reminders, find files and folders, and more.

▓ ▓ ▓

CHAPTER 7

Touch and Alternative Input Options

Touch is everywhere. There was a time, not long ago, when the idea of using touch as the sole method for interacting with a PC might have seemed outlandish. The popularity of smartphones and tablets, however, has proven not only that is touch here to stay, but also that we can do some pretty powerful things with it.

Using Windows 10 with Touch

In Chapter 3, I detailed the different touch and trackpad gestures available in Windows 10. There are a great many useful gestures here, including quickly being able to hide all your displayed apps and switch between them.

Windows 10 comes with accessibility features to help you interact with your PC using touch, but you should start with the touch features that you're already using. You may be surprised how useful these can be when it comes to making your PC easier to use.

The experience you get with touch in apps, both traditional Win32 desktop apps (such as Microsoft Office and Adobe Creative Suite) and Store apps, will vary, because different app developers support touch controls in different ways. In Microsoft's own apps, including the Edge browser, Internet Explorer, Microsoft Office (Word, Excel, PowerPoint, Outlook, OneNote, Access, Visio, and Publisher), and also Microsoft's Office Mobile Store apps (Word, Excel, PowerPoint, and OneNote), there is full touch integration.

If you've been using Microsoft Office and Internet Explorer for the last few years, you may have noticed the zoom control bar that sits in the bottom-right corner of the app window; refer to Figure 7-1.

Figure 7-1. *The zoom slider control sits in the bottom-right corner of Internet Explorer and Microsoft's Office suite*

You can move this slider to the left and right, or use the – and + buttons to its left or right, to make a web page or your documents larger or smaller onscreen.

■ **Tip**   You can also zoom into and out of documents in Microsoft and some other apps by holding the Ctrl key and pressing – or + on your keyboard, or by holding the Ctrl key and moving the mouse wheel back and forward.

With touch, you can also use pinch gestures to make your documents appear smaller or larger onscreen. To do this, put two fingers on your touchscreen, and move them together (to make the document smaller) or away from one another (to make the document larger).

■ **Tip**   Pinch-zoom gestures also work on the trackpads of many, but not all, laptops.

If you have difficulty using a physical keyboard, tapping in a text-entry field or in a blank space in a document in an app displays in onscreen keyboard, which I described in Chapter 5. Depending on the app, you can also use touch to drag and drop items in documents, highlight things onscreen, and select items. I talk more about making apps more accessible in Chapter 6.

There are three edge swipes you can perform in Windows 10 that can make working with your apps much easier. Place your finger on the screen bezel and swipe inward, toward the center of the screen, in a single movement:

- *Swiping inward from the left of the screen* displays the Task view, in which large, easy-to-identify thumbnail images of your running apps appear. You can tap an app to switch to it.

- *Swiping inward from the right of the screen* displays the Action Center, in which you can see notifications from your apps and Windows and get quick access to features such as Wi-Fi, Quiet Mode, and Screen Brightness using the quick access buttons in the bottom-right of the screen.

- *Swipe inward from the top of the screen* performs two actions. If you swipe from the very top of the screen to the very bottom, the currently running app is closed. If you swipe from the top of the screen to the center-left or center-right, you can dock your app to the left or right side of the screen. Thumbnail images of your other running apps then appear in the other half of the screen, and you can tap one to make it fill that remaining space. If you do not have another running app, open the Start menu, and the next app you run will automatically fill the remaining space.

Windows 10 Touch and Trackpad Gestures

If you use a laptop or tablet, you already use touch to control some aspects of Windows 10. On laptops, the touch gestures can vary slightly from one manufacturer to another, because a few companies implement their own touch gestures. But the standard gestures that work with any Windows 10 laptop or tablet can be extremely useful; refer to Table 7-1.

Table 7-1. *Windows 8 Touch Gestures*

Touch Gesture	Command	Action
Tap	Click	Tap the screen with your finger.
Double tap	Double-click	Tap the screen twice in the same place with your finger.
Drag vertically	Scroll	Touch the screen, and vertically drag your finger upward or downward.
Drag horizontally	Drag selection	Touch the screen, and horizontally drag your finger left or right.
Press and hold	Right-click	Touch and hold the screen with one finger while tapping it briefly with another finger.
Zoom	Zoom	Move two fingers apart (zoom in) or toward each other (zoom out).
Rotate	Rotate	Move two fingers in a circular motion.
Two-finger tap	Programmable in some apps	Tap the screen with two fingers.
Flick	Pan up, down, back, forward	Flick your finger up, down, left, or right on the screen.

Narrator Touch Gestures

I discussed the Narrator in detail in Chapter 3. But for the sake of keeping gestures together in the same place, Table 7-2 lists all the touch gestures that can be used to control the Narrator feature in Windows 10.

Table 7-2. Narrator Touch Gestures

Touch Gesture	Command
Tap or drag.	Read aloud the item under your finger.
Double tap, or hold with one finger and tap with a second finger.	Activate an item (equivalent to a single mouse click).
Triple tap, or hold with one finger and double-tap with a second finger.	Select an item.
Flick left or right.	Move to the next or previous item.
Hold with one finger, and two-finger-tap with additional fingers.	Drag an item.
Two-finger tap.	Stop the Narrator from speaking.
Two-finger swipe.	Scroll.
Three-finger tap.	Show or hide the Narrator Settings window.
Three-finger swipe up.	Read the current window.
Three-finger swipe down.	Read from the current text location.
Three-finger swipe left or right.	Tab forward and backward.
Four-finger tap.	Show all commands for the current item.
Four-finger triple tap.	Show the Narrator commands list.
Four-finger swipe up or down.	Enable/disable semantic zoom (semantic zoom provides a view of large blocks of content—on a web site, for example).

Using and Training Handwriting Recognition

If you have a laptop or tablet that supports a stylus, such as a Microsoft Surface, then handwriting recognition is an option for you. In many ways, it is easier and more natural than using a keyboard, and you can be much less precise. This is because whereas a keyboard forces you to type a specific way (the keys are all a set size and in a set place), you can train the handwriting-recognition system in Windows 10 to respond correctly to the way you write.

You can find the pen controls in the Devices section of the Settings app: Pen is listed in the left panel. There are three options; refer to Figure 7-2.

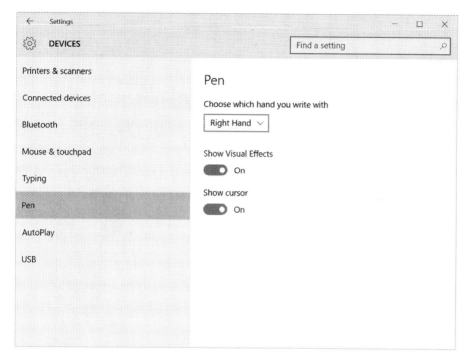

Figure 7-2. *The pen options are a drop-down box in which to choose Left Hand or Right Hand and Show Visual Effects and Show Cursor, both of which are toggle switches*

A drop-down box is your first choice, asking if you are left-handed or right-handed. Below this are toggle switches to show/hide handwriting visual effects that can highlight your pen usage onscreen and show/hide the cursor.

You can train the handwriting recognition in Windows 10 through the Control Panel. The quickest way to access the correct setting is to search in the Start menu or in Cortana for **Language** and selecting Language ➤ Control Panel when it appears in the search results; refer to Figure 7-3.

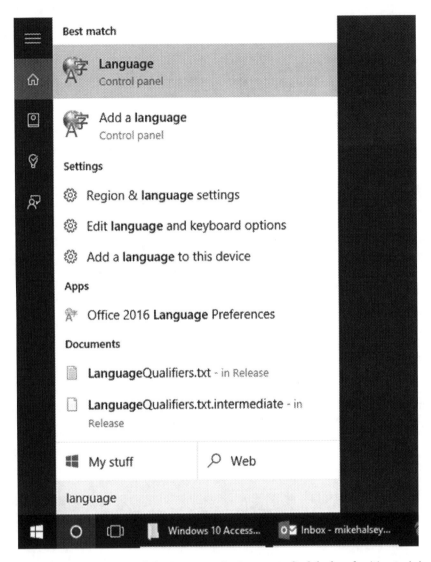

Figure 7-3. *You can search for **Language** in Cortana to find the handwriting training option*

When the Language options are open, select the Options link to the right of your installed language. All installed languages appear in a vertical list; refer to Figure 7-4.

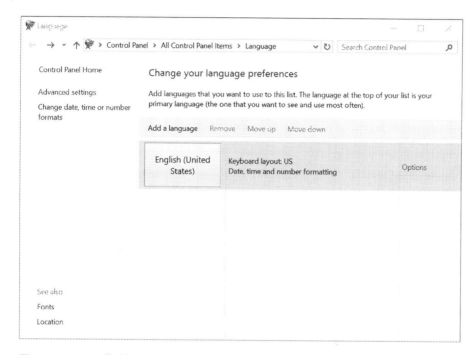

Figure 7-4. *Installed languages appear in a list, each with an Options link to its right*

Choose Options. On the next screen, near bottom left in the window, you see a Personalize Handwriting Recognition link. Select this to open a wizard that you can use to train Windows 10 to recognize your handwriting. With the Handwriting Personalization window open, you have two options available; refer to Figure 7-5:

- *Target Specific Recognition Errors*: Useful if Windows 10 generally recognizes your handwriting but some errors (perhaps the way you write specific numbers or letters) keep creeping in

- *Teach The Recognizer Your Handwriting Style*: Checks whether your handwriting is not being easily recognized by Windows 10

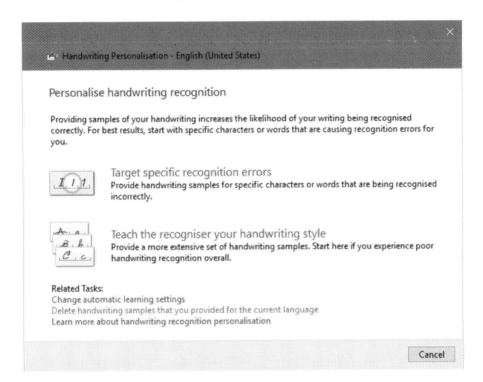

Figure 7-5. *The Handwriting Personalization window presents two options as buttons*

When you want to train Windows 10 to filter out specific character errors, you are again presented with two options; refer to Figure 7-6.

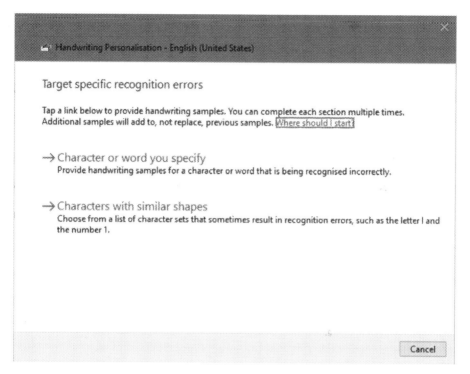

Figure 7-6. *Training Windows 10 to filter out specific character errors gives you two options: Character Or Word You Specify and, below that, Characters With Similar Shapes*

The first of these options, Character Or Word You Specify, asks you to enter the character or word you wish to train, using the onscreen keyboard. Selecting the next button displays an input box where you are asked to write the specific character or word several times; refer to Figure 7-7.

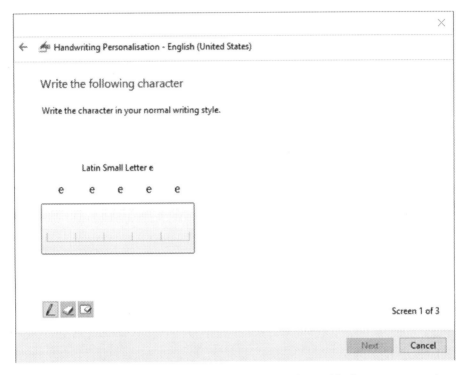

Figure 7-7. *You can train Windows 10 to recognize errors in specific characters or words*

If you choose the option to train Windows 10 to recognize Characters With Similar Shapes, you see a vertical list of available options in your language; refer to Figure 7-8.

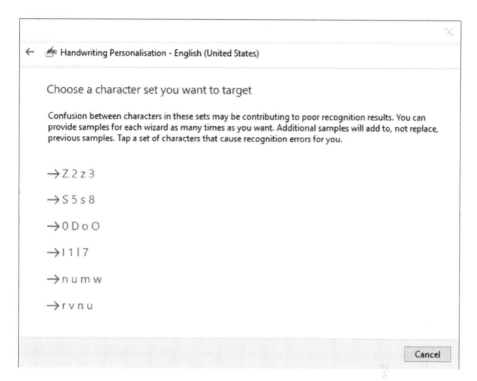

Figure 7-8. *Training Windows 10 to recognize characters written with similar shapes presents a vertical list of character groups in your language*

Selecting one these options walks you through each character, asking you to write each one five times; refer to Figure 7-9.

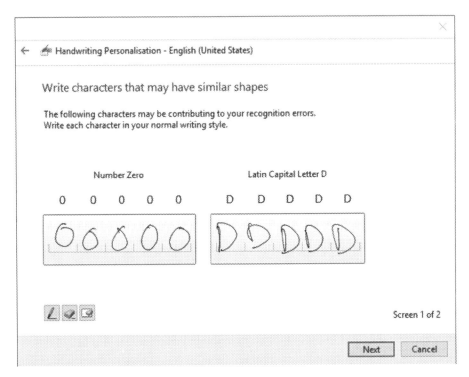

Figure 7-9. *You are asked, on several pages, to write each of the similarly shaped characters five times. Selecting the Next button near the bottom-right corner of the window to move from page to page*

Once you have trained your Windows 10 PC to recognize your handwriting, you can use the handwriting input panel I described in Chapter 5, which is available on the onscreen keyboard; refer to Figure 7-10.

Figure 7-10. *The handwriting input panel is available as part of the Windows 10 onscreen keyboard*

Using Speech Recognition in Windows 10

In Chapter 9, I discuss how you can use Cortana to dictate e-mails and control your PC with your voice. You can use many more voice commands with your PC, and the settings can be found in the Speech section of the Time & Language settings.

In the Speech settings, scroll down the page until you get to the Microphone Get Started button. Select it to set up your microphone for speech recognition; refer to Figure 7-11.

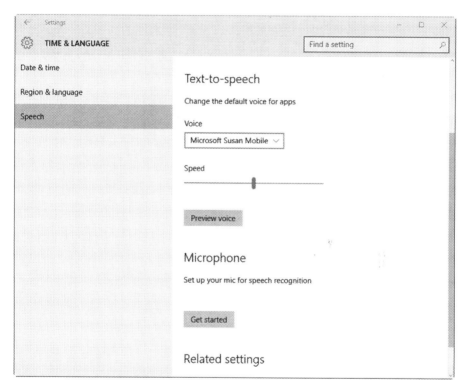

Figure 7-11. *To use speech recognition on your PC, you need to train Windows 10 to identify your voice*

To train your PC, you are asked to read a sentence aloud and given confirmation when you have been understood.

The Windows Speech Recognition app is not part of the Ease of Access tools and can be found by searching for **Speech** in the Start menu or Cortana. You are asked what microphone you wish to use, and you may be asked to read a sentence aloud again.

During setup of speech recognition you are asked to choose an activation mode; refer to Figure 7-12.

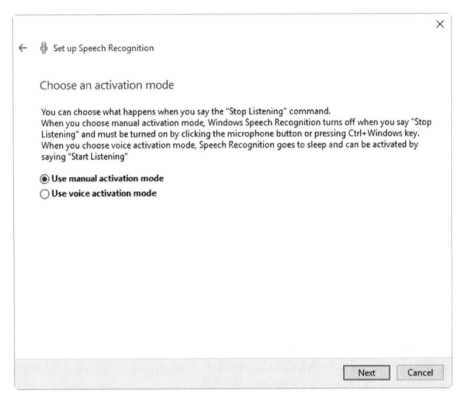

Figure 7-12. You are asked if you want to activate speech recognition manually or by using your voice

If you choose manual activation, you need to run Windows Speech Recognition whenever you want to use it. If you choose voice activation, however, you can activate and deactivate the feature by saying "Start listening" and "Stop listening."

When activated, Windows Speech Recognition is docked to the top-center of your screen; refer to Figure 7-13. You can drag it and place it anywhere you want.

Figure 7-13. *Windows Speech Recognition starts docked to the top-center of your screen*

You can use various commands with Windows Speech Recognition:

- *"Start,"* followed by the name of an app, such as "Calculator," "Word," or "PowerPoint."

- *"Switch to,"* followed by the name of an open app to switch to.

- *"[Menu name]"*: If you speak the name of a drop-down menu, that menu in an app opens for you. This also works to switch between tabs on ribbon interfaces in Windows and Office.

- *"Show numbers"* displays numbers overlaid on controls in an app; refer to Figure 7-14. You can then speak a number to activate that control.

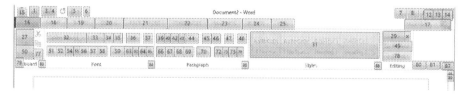

Figure 7-14. *The "Show numbers" command overlays numbers on buttons in an app interface; you can then speak a number to activate a control*

- *"[Link Name]"*: When you are reading a web page, you can activate a link by speaking its name.

- *"Double-click" and "Right-click"* can be used with the name of an app: for example, "Double-click Recycle bin."

- *"Start listening" and "Stop listening"* can be used (if activated) to turn speech recognition on and off, respectively.

- *"What can I say?"* displays a list of voice commands you can use with your PC.

- *"Show speech options"* displays a pop-up menu containing controls for the speech-recognition system in Windows 10.

- *"Hide Speech Recognition" and "Show Speech Recognition"* minimize and display the Speech Recognition widget, respectively.

95

If the Speech Recognition system doesn't understand what you're saying, it does one of two things. It may display a small edit box at the current cursor point (refer to Figure 7-15), in which you can type what you meant to say.

Figure 7-15. *An edit box may appear if the Speech Recognition system doesn't understand you. You can type in the box to train the recognizer*

Alternatively, it may present a list of alternative words of phrases; refer to Figure 7-16. Say the number next to the correct one to select it, or select Cancel if none are correct.

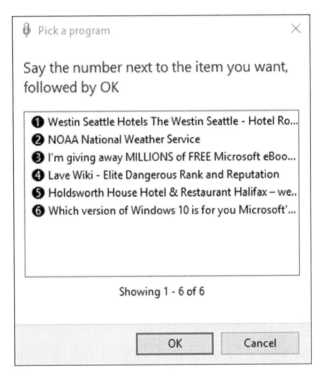

Figure 7-16. *You may be presented with a list of alternatives. Say the number next to the correct one*

Summary

There are several different ways to interact with your PC. Touch and handwriting can feel natural and make this interaction less stressful. With the smaller screen of a Windows 10 Mobile smartphone, you don't need to worry about accessibility options, though, because the Ease of Access features available on your PC are also available on the phone.

Touch is a very natural way to interact with a PC, but being able to speak to your PC and dictate items—even entire documents—can make the PC significantly easier to use. This chapter explained how you can use Cortana with speech, and Chapter 9 goes into this in more detail.

CHAPTER 8

■ ■ ■

Managing Accessibility on Windows 10 Mobile

The benefit of smartphones in our lives is a real, measurable metric. Being able to get instant access to the Internet, e-mail, instant messaging, GPS mapping, and a wealth of other information through apps can make anyone's life easier and simpler.

There's a downside to using smartphones, however: the limited screen size available can make text and other items difficult to see and read. Buttons and the onscreen keyboard can also be extremely fiddly to use, especially if you have problems with coordination.

Windows 10 Mobile smartphones come with some very useful accessibility tricks up their sleeve, though, not the least of which is that because they run the full version of Windows 10, all the settings and options are in the same places as on a desktop PC or laptop.

Accessibility Features on Windows 10 Mobile

You access the main settings screen in Windows 10 Mobile by swiping downward from the top of the screen to open the Action Center and then selecting the All Settings button near top right on the display; refer to Figure 8-1.

Figure 8-1. *You access settings in Windows 10 Mobile by swiping downward from the top of the screen and then selecting the All Settings button near top right on the display, just under the clock and the battery indicator*

In the Settings app, you see Ease Of Access listed in the seventh position; refer to Figure 8-2.

Figure 8-2. *The Settings app displays each category in a vertical list. Ease of Access is the seventh option on that list*

The Ease of Access options are very similar to those in the desktop Windows 10 Settings app. They are split into five main areas, all in a vertical list onscreen; refer to Figure 8-3.

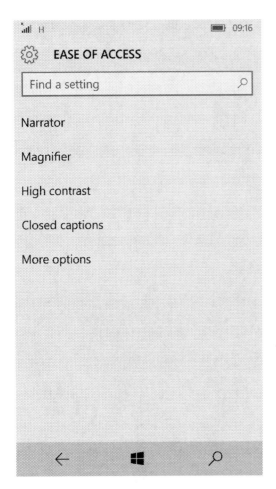

Figure 8-3. The Ease of Access options are presented in a vertical list: top to bottom, they are Narrator, Magnifier, High Contrast, Closed Captions, and More Options

Narrator

The first Ease of Access option is using the Narrator. I talk about the Narrator in more depth in Chapter 5, but the controls available in Windows 10 Mobile are as follows (refer to Figure 8-4):

- *Narrator On/Off*: A toggle switch to turn the feature on or off

- *Narrator Quick Launch*: A toggle switch that allows you to activate the Narrator by pressing and holding the Volume Up button on your device

- *Voice*: A drop-down menu that lets you o choose a female or male voice for the Narrator

- *Speed*: A horizontal slider you can use to speed up or slow down the Narrator's voice

- *Sounds You Hear*: Two toggle switches, one above the other—Read Hints for Controls and Buttons, and Play Audio Cues.

- *Cursor and Keys*: Two toggle switches, one above the other—Have Insertion Point [such as the cursor] Follow Narrator, and Activate Keys On Touch Keyboard When I Lift My finger Off The Keyboard

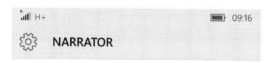

Hear text and controls on the screen

Narrator

 Off

Narrator is a screen reader that reads all the elements on screen, like text and buttons.

Narrator quick launch

 Off

When this setting is turned on, pressing and holding the Volume Up button and then pressing the start button will turn the Narrator on

Voice

Figure 8-4. *The Narrator options include turning it on or off via the Quick Launch method or pressing and holding the Volume Up button*

Magnifier

The Magnifier is a simple on/off toggle switch; refer to Figure 8-5. When it's activated, you can double-tap with two fingers on your screen, and the screen is magnified at that position. Now you use two-finger swipe gestures to move around the screen, because it's not all displayed at once, and double-tap with two fingers again to return to the regular screen view.

Magnify things on the screen

Screen magnifier

 Off

To magnify, double-tap with two fingers. To pan while magnified, use two fingers. To change zoom level while magnified, use two fingers to double-tap and hold, then pan up or down.

Figure 8-5. *The Magnifier makes items on your screen larger when you double-tap with two fingers*

High Contrast

High Contrast is, again, a simple on/off toggle switch; refer to Figure 8-6. Turning on this feature increases the contrast in the colors of foreground and background items, making things easier to see and read on your screen.

Choose a theme

High Contrast

 Off

Changes the colours for some features, and hides some of their background images.

Figure 8-6. Turning on the High Contrast color scheme can make your screen and items on it easier to read

Closed Captions

Just like a desktop, laptop, or tablet PC, your smartphone can display closed-captioning subtitles when video is played through compatible apps, such as the Microsoft Movies & TV app; refer to Figure 8-7.

Figure 8-7. Video played on a Windows 10 Mobile smartphone can have closed-captioning support

The options available for closed captioning include being able to specify the color, transparency, style, and size of captions onscreen. These options are all displayed as drop-down menus.

Below these are additional options you can use to select the background and window colors and transparency for the closed captions. At the top of the Closed Captions window, a live preview of the current settings is always displayed.

More Options

In the More Options section is a horizontal slider you can use to specify the scaling size for text on your smartphone screen; refer to Figure 8-8.

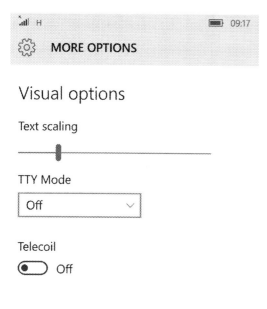

Figure 8-8. *You can use Text Scaling to make text on your smartphone easier to read. This operates via a horizontal slider*

Moving this slider to the right (it goes up to 200%) makes the text larger and easier to read in Windows 10 Mobile features and all of your installed apps. Figure 8-9 shows an example of two Settings screens: the one on the left is at normal size (100%), and the one on the right is at 200% size.

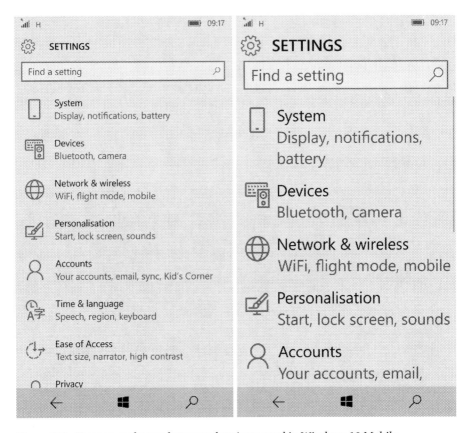

Figure 8-9. *You can make text larger and easier to read in Windows 10 Mobile*

If you need the TTY text phone service, a drop-down box to activate this is also available in the More Options panel.

Using the Onscreen Keyboard in Windows 10 Mobile

Although the text-scaling option in Windows 10 Mobile makes text onscreen larger and easier to read, it doesn't make the onscreen keyboard any bigger. This is because of the physical constraints of showing a full keyboard on the width of a smartphone screen.

You can choose from three keyboard sizes in Settings under Time & Language and Keyboard. Select the More Keyboard Settings button to display a drop-down menu in which you can choose a small, medium, or large keyboard—but on a small smartphone screen, even the large keyboard (which is the one I use, because I have fat fingers) isn't huge.

As an alternative to using the keyboard, and without having to activate any settings, look for the Microphone icon at top left on the Windows 10 Mobile keyboard; refer to Figure 8-10. You can select this icon to dictate into your device's microphone, rather than having to type. This can be useful if you have difficulty using the small keyboard.

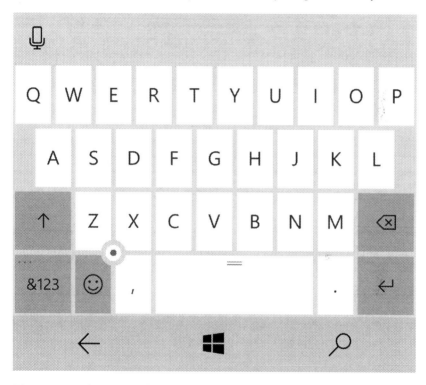

Figure 8-10. *The onscreen keyboard in Windows 10 Mobile includes a microphone icon in the top-left corner that allows you to speak to the device instead of type*

Summary

There are several different ways to interact with your PC. Touch and handwriting can feel natural and make this interaction less stressful. With the smaller screen of a Windows 10 Mobile smartphone, you don't need to worry about accessibility options, though: the Ease of Access features available on your PC are also available on the phone. This includes being able to speak to dictate e-mails and messages. Additionally, all the features of Cortana that I detailed in Chapter 3 are available, which can make using a Windows 10 Mobile smartphone a much easier and more enjoyable experience.

CHAPTER 9

Windows 10 Usability Tips and Tricks

Throughout this book, I've shown you how to get the very best from the accessibility features in Windows 10, whoever you are and whatever your needs. I want to finish by looking at some additional things you can do and ways in which you can use the accessibility features to achieve more, and work more productively on your PC.

Using Cortana to Boost Your Productivity

So what are all these cool things you can do with Cortana? Saying "Hey Cortana, tell me a joke" or "... sing me a song" is all right for an occasional distraction, but you need to get things done on your PC.

Here are some of the things you can do with Cortana. Remember, this functionality will be expanded over time, so it's worth experimenting with new phrases:

Launch [app name] is a quick way to open apps on your PC. When you ask Cortana to launch an app, such as PowerPoint (refer to Figure 9-1), you get both audible and visible feedback about what action Cortana is performing, so you can check whether she misheard you.

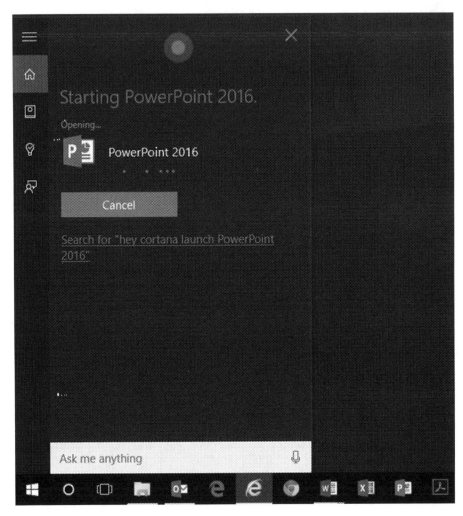

Figure 9-1. *Saying "Hey Cortana, launch PowerPoint" opens Microsoft PowerPoint (if installed) on your PC. Cortana gives you both audible and visible feedback about what she is doing*

Remind me is a wonderfully flexible tool for keeping your workflow going while setting reminders for appointments, tasks, and more. You can tell Cortana to remind you about anything, such as "Pick up some flowers," as in Figure 9-2.

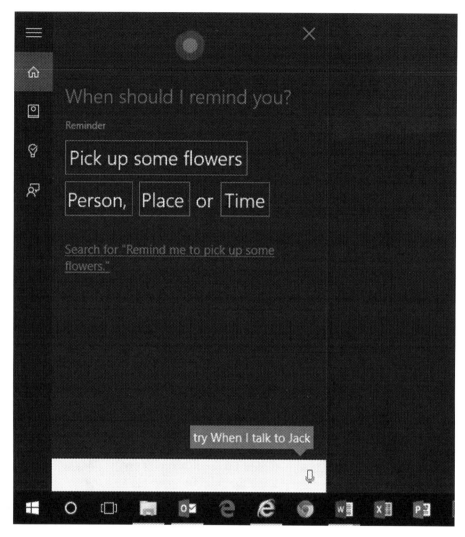

Figure 9-2. *You can set all aspects of reminders using your voice, and Cortana provides visible and audible feedback at every stage. If she mishears something, then when she asks for confirmation, say "No"; she'll ask you for the correct information*

Reminders can be set by person, place, or time. You can be reminded, for example, when you're having a meeting with a specific person, are going to or are arriving at a specific place (more on this shortly), or at a specified time.

In Cortana's settings, you can set locations such as Home and Work, but you can also specify locations by street address. "Remind me to pick up the dry cleaning the next time I'm on High Street, Sheffield" sets a location-based reminder that will alert you when you're in the vicinity of that place.

If you sign in to your Windows 10 devices using a Microsoft account, Azure Active Directory, or Domain account that can synchronize your settings, Cortana also syncs between those devices (if she's been activated on each one). This means you can set a reminder on your desktop PC and be later reminded on your smartphone or tablet. It's a very clever feature.

As I have already mentioned, if Cortana mishears you, it's not a problem because you get both audible and visible feedback of what you've told her to do. When she asks if something is okay, just say "No," and you'll be asked to clarify what she got wrong; refer to Figure 9-3.

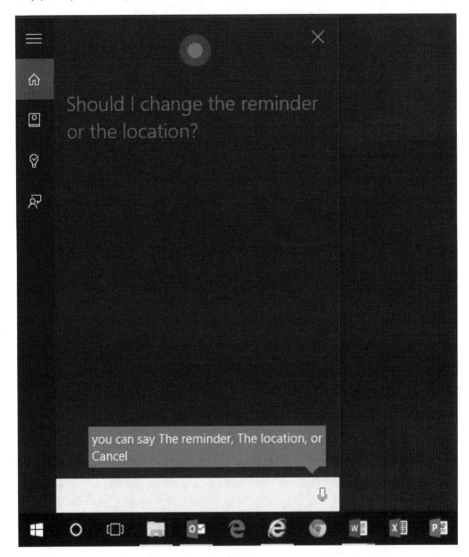

Figure 9-3. *If you want to change anything because Cortana misheard you, say "No" when she asks if everything is okay. You'll be asked what she got wrong*

Find all my can perform an instant, global search for documents, pictures, videos, and more and display the results in an easy-to-navigate Cortana window; refer to Figure 9-4.

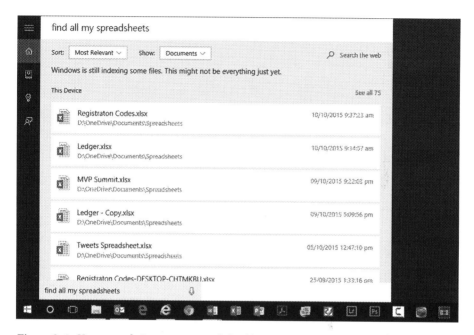

Figure 9-4. *You can ask Cortana to search for files, and they appear in a scrollable list in the Cortana window*

Send an e-mail to can be used to dictate e-mails and Skype messages, and other Windows store apps that can integrate with Cortana). You can speak the subject and full message text, and at every stage you receive audible and visible feedback; refer to Figure 9-5.

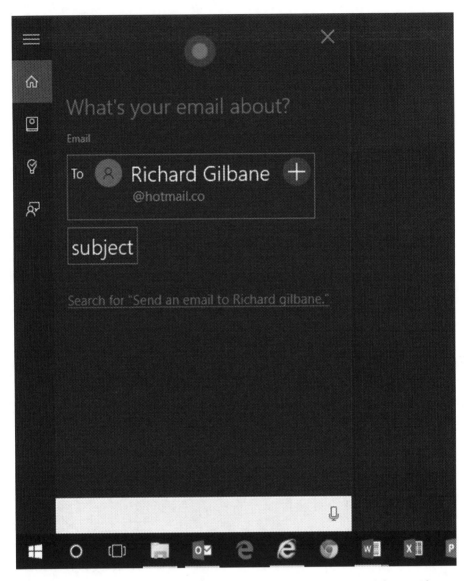

Figure 9-5. *You can dictate e-mails and instant messages in Cortana, and she provides audible and visible feedback at every stage*

Other useful functions with Cortana include the following:

- *What appointments do I have today?*

- *What's the weather doing tomorrow?*

- *Show me messages from*

- *Wake me up in half an hour*

- *Set an alarm for*

- *Get me driving directions to*

- *Where am I?*

- *Show me the headlines / sports news*

- *Take a note*

- *Turn on / off Wi-Fi*

- *What's the status of American Airlines flight 534?*

- *What's the status of my parcel from UPS?*

When you speak one of these commands, the results come back to you in speech, so news, sports, and business headlines are read aloud.

Making Search Easier

You can use Cortana to aid with search, but we all spend time using Microsoft's Bing or Google to find what we need online, and searching our PCs for files and documents. I want to share with you my top tips for maximizing search in Windows 10.

Improving Internet Searches

Searching online can be a frustrating experience. With many millions of web sites reported in the average search, and additional challenges because you aren't able to properly read or interact with the search page, finding what you need can sometimes be exasperating.

Here are some tips you can follow to make your online searches more targeted. These tips work with all the major search engines:

- "Enclosing a phrase in double quotes" forces a search for that entire phrase.

- Putting a plus (+) symbol in front of a word forces the search engine to only return results that definitely contain that exact word.

- Putting a minus (-) symbol in front of a word excludes any searches that include that word.

- You can search for results from a specific web site by adding
  `site:sitename.com` to your search.

- Wildcard operators can be used if you're unsure of the spelling of
  a word. A star (*) represents a series of characters, as in "Mike H*"
  and a question mark (?) represents a single character, as in "Mike
  H?alsey".

- You can include the words *and, or,* and *not* to narrow your search
  results: for example, "Microsoft Surface 2016 or 2017".

Searching Your PC

Cortana is a really useful tool to use to search your PC, because it includes voice control.
Sometimes you need additional power for your searches, especially if, like me, you have
many thousands of files and photos.

You can search in File Explorer by selecting the search box on the very right in the
window, below the Ribbon; refer to Figure 9-6.

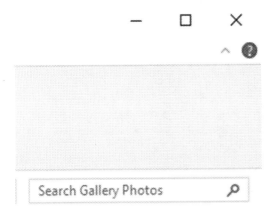

Figure 9-6. *The search box in File Explorer can be found near the top-right corner of the
window, just below the Ribbon menu*

When you select the search box, the Ribbon changes to offer context-sensitive options in drop-down menus; refer to Figure 9-7.

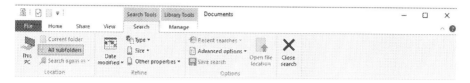

Figure 9-7. *A Search tab appears on the File Explorer Ribbon when you search, with options available as drop-down menus*

Using these drop-down options can greatly improve the quality of your searches by reducing them to specific file types or file sizes or specifying when the file was created or last modified.

You can also use text commands in the search box to narrow your searches further:

- *Type:=image* or *Type:=.pdf* searches for a specific type of file, in this case an image or an Adobe Acrobat Portable Document Format (PDF) file.

- *Name:keyword* searches within documents and their saved names for a specific keyword, such as *budget, wedding,* or vacation.

Using Saved Searches to Improve Search on Your PC

Speaking of recently modified files, you may find that you're working on a project but that the files for that project are scattered in various places on your PC. For example, they may include pictures and documents that are not stored together.

Once you have performed a search in File Explorer—for example, for a keyword relevant to all files, such as *Name:Contoso*—select the Save Seach button on the Ribbon; refer to Figure 9-8.

Figure 9-8. *You can save your searches for later reference by selecting the Save Search button on the Ribbon*

119

When asked where you want to save the search, select your Desktop, either from the Desktop link in the Quick Access panel to the left of the File Explorer Window or by selecting the arrow next to your name in the top-left corner of the Save As dialog; refer to Figure 9-9.

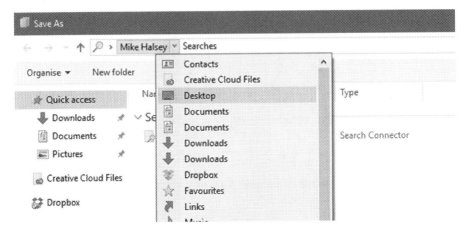

Figure 9-9. *You can save searches directly to the Desktop by selecting the arrow to the right of your name in the top-left corner of the Save As dialog, and selecting Desktop from the options that appear in a drop-down menu*

The search now appears as an icon on your desktop where you can double-click or double-tap it to reopen the search. It's worth noting that this search is not static, and it will automatically update with the latest file information every time it is opened.

Making It Easier to Use Apps

In Chapter 6, I explained how you can use features in Windows 10 to make it easier to focus on your apps to help maximize your productivity. I want to highlight a few of these features again, because they are extremely useful. I also show how you can use them in environments such as distracting or noisy workplaces.

In the Ease of Access settings, select Other Options for some useful tools to help you concentrate (refer to Figure 9-10):

- *Play Animations In Windows*: Lets you disable all the visible animations on your PC, such as the ones when apps open, close, or are minimized.

- *Show Windows Background*: Lets you hide your desktop wallpaper picture, replacing it with a plain black screen.

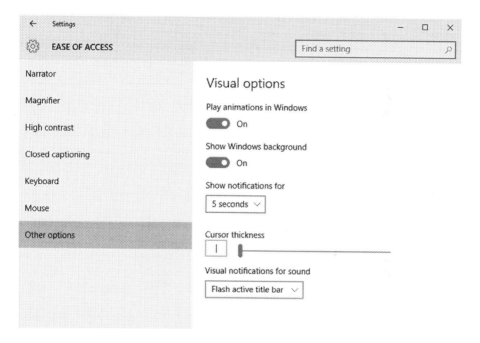

Figure 9-10. *Other Options in the Ease of Access settings can disable visible animations and your desktop wallpaper*

■ **Tip** On a smartphone, laptop, or tablet with an LED screen, black pixels do not draw any power, so having a plain black background can extend the battery life of your device.

- *Show Notifications For*: Extremely useful if toast notifications in Windows (so called because they pop up) disappear from your desktop before you can read them. You can change the setting for any length of time from 5 seconds to 5 minutes. You can manually dismiss each toast by selecting the close (X) button in its top-right corner.

- *Cursor Thickness*: Changes the thickness of your input cursor in apps such as e-mail and Microsoft Office, making it easier to see where the cursor is currently located.

- *Visual Notifications For Sound*: Flashes the title bar of an app, the entire app, or the entire desktop to alert you to a notification that is normally signaled through a sound. This can also be useful if you work in a very noisy environment.

Additionally, changing the scaling options for your desktop can make apps, text, and images considerably easier to see and read. In the Settings app, select System, and a slider appears. You can use it to change the size of text, apps, and other items; refer to Figure 9-11.

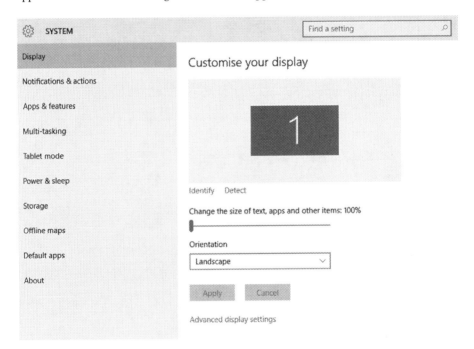

Figure 9-11. You can control the scaling of your desktop screen using a left-to-right slider control

This scaling works from 100% (the standard resolution of your monitor) up to 350% for compatible displays and can make everything significantly easier to see and read.

Windows 10 Shortcut Keys

You can speak to your Windows 10 PC to get things done, and you can also use a combination of keyboard shortcuts to achieve all manner of interesting and useful things. There are keys that can be used on their own and keys that can be used in combination with other keys, such as Ctrl, Alt, Shift, and the Windows key. You can even use keyboard shortcuts with your mouse wheel.

You may be most familiar with the Ctrl+X (Cut), Ctrl+C (Copy), Ctrl+V (Paste), and Ctrl+Alt+Del key combinations. Table 9-1 through Table 9-7 provide a full list of the keyboard shortcuts available in Windows 10. Some of these keyboard shortcuts can control accessibility aspects such as high-contrast color schemes and the Magnifier.

Table 9-1. *Keys with No Modifier*

Key	Function
Space	Select or clear the active check box.
Tab	Move forward through options.
Esc	Cancel.
NumLock	Hold for 5 seconds: Toggle Keys.
Del	Delete file (File Explorer).
Left arrow	Open the previous menu or close a submenu.
Right arrow	Open the next menu or open a submenu.
F1	Display help (if available).
F2	Rename an item.
F3	Search for the next instance in a search.
F4	Display items in the active list.
F5	Refresh.

Table 9-2. *Windows Logo Key Combinations*

Windows Logo Key+	Function
No other key	Toggle the Start screen/last app.
PrtScr	Capture a screenshot (saved in Pictures as screenshot.png, screenshot(1).png, screenshot(2).png, and so on).
C	Open Cortana.
D	Show the desktop.
E	Open File Explorer.
F	Open files in the Search charm (+Ctrl to find computers on a network).
H	Open the Share panel.
I	Open the Settings app.
J	Switch focus between snapped and larger apps.
K	Open the Connect To Devices panel
L	Switch users (lock the computer if on a domain).
M	Minimize all windows (desktop).
O	Change the lock-screen orientation.
P	Open the second screen and projection options.
Q	Open the Search charm.
R	Open the Run dialog box.
T	Set focus on the taskbar, and cycle through running desktop programs.
U	Open the Ease of Access Center.
V	Cycle through notifications (+Shift to go backward).
X	Quick-link power users' commands (open the Windows Mobility Center, if present).
Z	Open the App bar.
1-9	Go to the app at the position on the taskbar.
+	Zoom in (Magnifier).
-	Zoom out (Magnifier).
, (comma)	Peek at the desktop.
. (period)	Snap an app to the right (+Shift to snap to the left).
Enter	Open the Narrator.
Spacebar	Switch the input language and keyboard layout.
Tab	Cycle through the app history (use Ctrl to use the arrow keys).

(*continued*)

Table 9-2. *(continued)*

Windows Logo Key+	Function
Esc	Exit the Magnifier.
Home	Minimize non-active desktop windows.
PgUp	Move the Start screen to the left monitor.
PgDn	Move the Start screen to the right monitor.
Left arrow	Snap desktop windows to the left (+Shift to move to the left monitor).
Right arrow	Snap desktop windows to the right (+Shift to move to the right monitor).
Up arrow	Maximize the desktop window (+Shift to keep its width).
Down arrow	Restore/Minimize the desktop window (+Shift to keep its width).
F1	Open Windows Help and Support, or open Help in an App.

Table 9-3. *Ctrl Key Combinations*

Ctrl+	Function
Mouse wheel	Desktop: change icon size; Start screen: zoom in/out.
A	Select All.
C	Copy.
E	Select the search box (Explorer).
N	Open a new window (Explorer).
R	Refresh.
V	Paste.
W	Close the current window (Explorer).
X	Cut.
Y	Redo.
Z	Undo.
Esc	Open the Start screen.
NumLock	Copy.
Left arrow	Select the Previous word.
Right arrow	Select the Next word.
Up arrow	Select the Previous paragraph.
Down arrow	Select the Next paragraph.
F4	Close the active document.

Table 9-4. *Alt Key Combinations*

Alt+	Function
D	Select the Address bar (Explorer).
Enter	Open the Properties dialog box.
Spacebar	Open a shortcut menu.
Tab	Switch between apps.
Left arrow	Move to the previous folder (Explorer).
Up arrow	Go up one level (Explorer).
F4	Close the active item or app.

Table 9-5. *Shift Key Combinations*

Shift+	Function
No other key	Five times: Sticky Keys.
Tab	Move backward through options.
Esc	Open Task Manager.
NumLock	Paste.
Left arrow	Select a block of text.
Right arrow	Select a block of text.
Up arrow	Select a block of text.
Down arrow	Select a block of text.

Table 9-6. *Ctrl + Alt Key Combinations*

Ctrl + Alt+	Function
D	Toggle Docked mode (Magnifier).
I	Invert colors (Magnifier).
L	Toggle Lens mode (Magnifier).
Tab	Switch between apps using the arrow keys.

Table 9-7. *Alt + Shift Key Combinations*

Alt + Shift+	Function
PrtScr	Left Alt + left Shift + PrtScr: high contrast
NumLock	Left Alt + left Shift + NumLock: mouse keys

Summary

In my book *Beginning Windows 10* (Apress, 2015), I place a heavy focus on productivity and using tips and tricks to boost your workflow and to make your experience using Windows 10 happier on whatever device you use. If you've found the hints and tips here useful, then I suggest that *Beginning Windows 10* is a natural next step.

Throughout this book, however, I've covered everything you need to know to make Windows 10 easier to use and more accessible and to improve your experience with your PC, laptop, tablet, or smartphone. I sincerely hope you've found this information useful, and I would like to leave you with one more resource: the Microsoft accessibility web site. You can visit `www.microsoft.com/enable` to find additional hints and tips to help you use your PC to the max, as well as links to third-party accessibility help and resources.

Index

▓ Y, Z

Get the eBook for only $5!

Why limit yourself?

Now you can take the weightless companion with you wherever you go and access your content on your PC, phone, tablet, or reader.

Since you've purchased this print book, we're happy to offer you the eBook in all 3 formats for just $5.

Convenient and fully searchable, the PDF version enables you to easily find and copy code—or perform examples by quickly toggling between instructions and applications. The MOBI format is ideal for your Kindle, while the ePUB can be utilized on a variety of mobile devices.

To learn more, go to www.apress.com/companion or contact support@apress.com.

Printed in the United States
By Bookmasters